Management Extra

EFFECTIVE COMMUNICATIONS

ELSEVIER eLEARN Pergamon *Flexible* Learning

AMSTERDAM • BOSTON • HEIDELBERG • LONDON • NEW YORK • OXFORD • PARIS •
SAN DIEGO • SAN FRANCISCO • SINGAPORE • SYDNEY • TOKYO

Pergamon Flexible Learning is an imprint of Elsevier
Linacre House, Jordan Hill, Oxford OX2 8DP, UK
30 Corporate Drive, Suite 400, Burlington, MA 01803, USA

First edition 2007

Notice
No responsibility is assumed by the publisher for any injury and/or damage
to persons or property as a matter of products liability, negligence or
otherwise, or from any use or operation of any methods, products,
instructions or ideas contained in the material herein. Because of rapid
advances in the medical sciences, in particular, independent verification of
diagnoses and drug dosages should be made

British Library Cataloguing in Publication Data
A catalogue record for this book is available from the British Library

Library of Congress Cataloging-in-Publication Data
A catalog record for this book is availabe from the Library of Congress

ISBN–13: 978-0-08-046529-6
ISBN–10: 0-08-046529-3

For information on all Pergamon Flexible Learning publications visit
our web site at books.elsevier.com

Printed and bound in Italy

07 08 09 10 11 10 9 8 7 6 5 4 3 2 1

Contents

Activities

Figures

Tables

Series preface

Whether you are a tutor/trainer or studying management development to further your career, Management Extra provides an exciting and flexible resource helping you to achieve your goals. The series is completely new and up-to-date, and has been written to harmonise with the 2004 national occupational standards in management and leadership. It has also been mapped to management qualifications, including the Institute of Leadership & Management's middle and senior management qualifications at Levels 5 and 7 respectively on the revised national framework.

For learners, coping with all the pressures of today's world, Management Extra offers you the flexibility to study at your own pace to fit around your professional and other commitments. Suddenly, you don't need a PC or to attend classes at a specific time – choose when and where to study to suit yourself! And, you will always have the complete workbook as a quick reference just when you need it.

For tutors/trainers, Management Extra provides an invaluable guide to what needs to be covered, and in what depth. It also allows learners who miss occasional sessions to 'catch up' by dipping into the series.

This series provides unrivalled support for all those involved in management development at middle and senior levels.

Reviews of Management Extra

I have utilised the Management Extra series for a number of Institute of Leadership and Management (ILM) Diploma in Management programmes. The series provides course tutors with the flexibility to run programmes in a variety of formats, from fully facilitated, using a choice of the titles as supporting information, to a tutorial based programme, where the complete series is provided for home study. These options also give course participants the flexibility to study in a manner which suits their personal circumstances. The content is interesting, thought provoking and up-to-date, and, as such, I would highly recommend the use of this series to suit a variety of individual and business needs.

Martin Davies BSc(Hons) MEd CEngMIMechE MCIPD FITOL FInstLM
Senior Lecturer, University of Wolverhampton Business School

At last, the complete set of books that make it all so clear and easy to follow for tutor and student. A must for all those taking middle/senior management training seriously.

Michael Crothers, ILM National Manager

Connected

Communication has long been a hot topic. What makes it exciting in our age is the application of new media and the individual empowerment that comes with blogs, wikkis, and mobile technology, in other words our sense of connectedness. These don't come without their difficulties, but they present some very interesting opportunities.

The first theme in this book looks at connectedness, models of communication and the barriers to communication. No amount of technology can compensate for a poorly structured message; indeed, the technology itself can eventually become a barrier. As instant communications are now the norm, do we need to spend more time focusing on the message and our audience?

The following themes look in more detail at meetings, written communications, presentations and interviews. They introduce elements of communication theory and ask you to carry out activities to evaluate and practice your own skills.

Franklin D. Roosevelt said about public speaking

Be sincere; be brief; be seated.

Pithy and apposite, this is just the advice that most of us need to become more effective communicators. This book is underpinned by the three themes captured in Roosevelt's words.

◆ being yourself, not slavishly following conventions that have no place in effective communications,

◆ focusing on what's important for your audience and

◆ knowing when to stop – when does connectedness become an issue, when do you judge less is more?

Your objectives are to:

◆ understand how you can improve your communication skills

◆ evaluate organisational communication systems and the importance of knowledge management

◆ develop your skills for leading and participating in meetings

◆ produce clear written communications

◆ plan and deliver effective presentations

◆ explore and use a range of interviewing techniques.

1 · Making the connection

Communication is a complex managerial skill that is at the heart of your ability to form relationships and motivate your colleagues. It is also one of the most frequently cited problems in organisations and, if handled badly, can lead to breakdowns in the interaction between the organisation and its stakeholders.

> When dealing with people, remember you are not dealing with creatures of logic, but creatures of emotion.

Dale Carnegie

There are no shortage of ways to communicate open to us. We can remain connected to family, friends and to work to an unprecedented degree. Yet the effectiveness of communications comes back to understanding how messages are transmitted and received, the perceptions and emotions involved and the barriers to making that connection on a personal basis, and on an organisational level. In this section you will:

◆ review concepts and theories of communication

◆ assess the factors that commonly create barriers to effective communication

◆ examine the importance of connections and how people in your organisation connect with each other.

What is effective communication?

Here are two definitions that will help to clarify what makes communication effective.

Murdock and Scutt (2003) define the *purpose* of interpersonal communication as:

> The exchange of information, verbally and through bodily expression, between two or more people in order to influence the occurrence of action, ideas or thoughts, at work, in leisure or community pursuits, or in individuals' domestic lives.

Source: Murdock and Scutt (2003)

In their book *Understanding Information* Jonathan Liebenau and James Backhouse (1990) define the communication *process* thus:

> Communication is a process which involves at least two parties. This process can be characterised as a set of activities involving a sender with intentions to convey, a medium or channel for carrying signals, and a receiver who has the ability to interpret those signals.

Source: Liebenau and Backhouse (1990)

From these two definitions, certain factors about communication are clear:

- It involves both words and non-verbal signals.
- It influences people's actions and ideas.
- Every message requires a sender and recipient and a medium, or channel, through which it can be conveyed.
- Messages can be misunderstood if people are not on the same wavelength or perceptions vary.

Because we spend so much time in conversation with colleagues, however, we rarely step back and think about the purpose of individual communications – and consequently our messages sometimes get lost. When we connect with another person, what are we trying to achieve?

Murdock and Scutt (2003) suggest that we communicate with each other in order to:

- inform
- instruct
- motivate

- persuade

- encourage

- negotiate

- understand other people's views and ideas

- listen because we want to learn

- seek, receive and give counselling, information, advice, decisions, etc.

Models of the communication process

Many theorists have analysed the communication process in an attempt to understand how we interact with other people, and created models to present their theories.

The transmission model

Effective communication is a two-way process. Liebenau and Backhouse (1990) developed a model to illustrate this process.

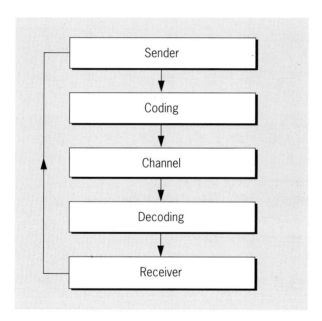

Figure 1.1 *Sending and receiving information*

There are a number of important features in this model.

- The sender chooses an appropriate medium or channel for the message – this could be face-to-face conversation, a phone conversation, email or the written word.

- The sender chooses a code for the message. This consists of language, words and body language that are appropriate for the receiver.

- The receiver decodes the message in order to interpret and understand it.

Liebenau and Backhouse's work is based on one of the first communication models developed by Claude Shannon and Warren Weaver in 1949. Shannon and Weaver were telephone engineers. Although they were principally concerned with communication *technology*, their model embodies the principles of human communication.

Shannon and Weaver suggested that messages could be distorted or lost because of external factors; in technological terms, they cited noise on telephone lines. This parallels the problems that can occur in interpersonal communications.

♦ The sender chooses an inappropriate code for the message so that it doesn't make sense to the receiver. For example, they may use language which is too complex or employ jargon.

♦ The receiver cannot decode the message because they don't possess the right 'vocabulary', or their own thoughts and preconceptions interfere with the message.

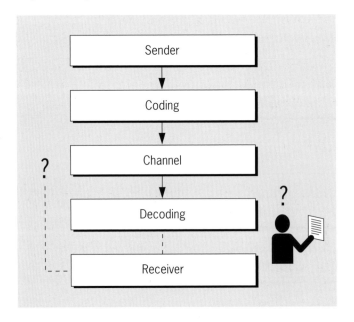

Figure 1.2 *The decoding transmission model*

The transmission model is useful for managers because it highlights where communication problems are most likely to arise, in the coding, the channel and the decoding by the receiver.

By encouraging you to think about the various components of the process, it encourages you to plan your communications, choose an appropriate medium and to pay attention to the needs of the person who is receiving your message.

Transactional analysis

In an ideal world, we would all think carefully about the way in which we communicate and choose appropriate codes and channels. In the real world, our communications are influenced by our personalities. Some of us find it easier to put our thoughts into words than others; sometimes the effectiveness of our communications are impeded by factors that we have difficulty in controlling, such as problems that we're experiencing that are unrelated to the message, aspects of our temperament, or our relationship with the receiver.

In the 1950s Eric Berne began to develop his theories of transactional analysis. He suggested that there are three distinct parts or 'ego states' to our personalities.

Berne suggested that when we code or receive a message, we do so from one of our ego states.

The Parent: these are the behaviours, attitudes, thoughts and feelings we have absorbed since we were young. They form our 'conditioning' and influence the way in which we respond to others.

The Child: these are the emotional responses that we have developed since childhood.

The Adult: this is our ability to think and decide what to do based on information that we've received rather than on conditioned, 'parental' responses or emotional 'childish' responses.

Figure 1.3 *The ego states of transactional analysis*

At the core of Berne's theory is the principle that effective transactions (i.e. successful communications) must be complementary. They must go back from the receiving ego state to the sending ego state. For example, if the sender is Parent to Child, the response must be Child to Parent, or the transaction is 'crossed', and there will be a problem between sender and receiver.

Source: www.businessballs.com

Berne's theories have been expanded over the years and have been applied to the management of communications. At a simple level, if two people are engaged in a dialogue and both are dominated by their 'child' ego state, then there is likely to be emotional meltdown. These diagrams show both complementary and crossed transactions.

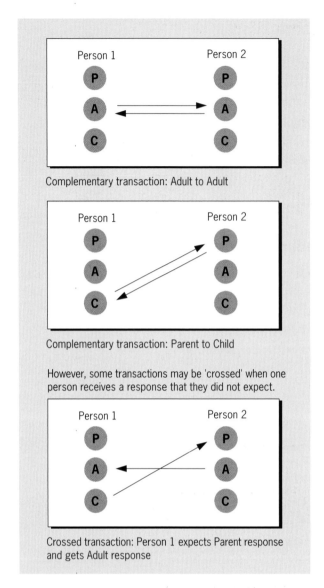

Figure 1.4 *Transactional analysis*

Many managers find that understanding the principles of transactional analysis helps them to understand the dynamics of workplace interaction. By recognizing both your own ego state and that of the receiver, you can amend your delivery to achieve effective communication.

Mark Twain captures the essence of the child to child miscommunication as follows.

> There is nothing so annoying as to have two people talking when you're busy interrupting.

Mark Twain

We communicate in various ways: through the spoken word and in writing; using words and non-verbal signals; electronically and face-to-face. Next you'll consider the key features of these different methods.

Types of communication

The boundaries between the types of communication we use are being blurred by technology. Consider instant messaging, essentially a written form of communication. Writing is generally expected to be considered and composed, however, the instantaneousness of the messages makes us more tolerant of mistakes and opinions expressed. We use smiley faces or emoticons to help us express our emotions and to overcome some of the difficulties of communicating in this way. This media explicitly attempts to use two different kinds of communication, verbal and non-verbal.

Verbal communication

Verbal communication is the words we say (or write down) when we communicate. Ironically, although words are the code by which our message is conveyed, many of us struggle to find the right words; we simply can't use the code properly.

There are five essential skills that enhance our ability to use the code and employ words effectively.

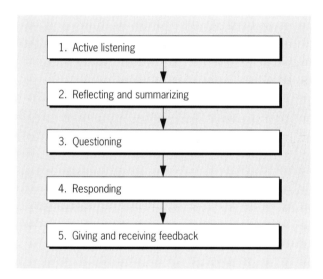

Figure 1.5 *Practising the skills of communication*

1   Active listening

A good communicator recognizes that you need to listen in order to understand where another person is coming from. Active listening involves trying to understand what the other person is saying, showing that you are listening, and periodically checking your understanding by asking questions, or for confirmation.

> **Minds are like parachutes – they only function when open.**
> **Thomas Dewar**

Barker (2000) suggests that communication is 'the process of creating shared understanding'. Active listening helps us to achieve this by encouraging us to step into the other person's shoes, thus learning more about their viewpoint and minimizing the barriers that are created by differing perceptions.

To listen actively:

◆ focus on the other person and turn off your internal dialogues. Many of us stop listening half-way through a sentence because we're already preparing our response

◆ avoid interrupting or changing the subject – let the other person keep control

◆ imagine their viewpoint – how do you think they are feeling, what are they experiencing, what do you know about their values?

◆ keep the focus on them; don't continually refer to your own experience or knowledge

◆ respond affirmatively – don't criticise or judge

◆ create rapport using non-verbal signals: maintain eye contact; sit forward, mirror their body language

◆ ask questions and reflect back what the other person has said to check your understanding.

It is also important to 'listen between the lines'. Sometimes you will pick up messages through non-verbal signals, or observe gaps in the other person's words, that suggest what they are really thinking.

'Communication in Britain is often about what people don't say, rather than what they do. Uniquely in our country, a manager can interpret his subordinate's silence as assent, while they see it as their ultimate protest.'

Source: John Harvey Jones, *Manage to Survive*, quoted in *The Dictionary of Business Quotations* (1996)

2 Reflecting and summarizing

Reflection provides useful opportunities to check understanding. Barker (2000) believes that restating the other person's ideas in your own language shows that you:

◆ recognize the points they have made

◆ appreciate the position from which they say it

◆ understand the beliefs that inform that position.

Summarising draws together the views of both parties. It is a useful way to periodically check on points that have been made or agreed.

3 Questioning

Questioning is another skill that helps us to understand what people are thinking.

Barker (2000) suggests that questions should be used to:

◆ find out facts

◆ check understanding

◆ help the other person improve their understanding

◆ invite the other person to examine your own thinking

◆ request action.

Here is an overview of some of the most frequently used questions types.

Question type	Description	Uses	Example
Closed	Can be answered with 'yes' or 'no' or single words	To focus discussions or get specific information	Can you attend the meeting on the 25th? How old are you?
Open	Cannot be answered with 'yes' or 'no' or single words	To broaden a discussion/get another person talking	What did your team do to respond to the change?
Leading	Suggests the answer	To influence	Wouldn't the best solution be to speed up delivery time?
Controlling	Influences the response	To take the lead in a conversation/discussion	Shall we finish here and move on to the next point?
Probing	Enquires deeper than previous questions	To elicit further information	Can you explain how the system works?
Reflective	Restates the question to the sender	To encourage a person to suggest a solution	So you think recruiting more people is the best option for achieving the new target?
Redirected	Restates the question to another person	To draw in a person who could make a useful contribution	Alex. you've raised a good point – Sarah, what do you think we should do next?
Overhead	Restates the question to the whole group	To invite anyone to respond and to move away from one person dominating the discussion	Alex has raised an interesting point – what do the rest of you think we should do next?
'What if'	Identifies potential blocks in the other person's thinking and seeks to find a solution	To encourage people to take a wider perspective	How would you proceed if you had more staff to deal with telephone queries?

Table 1.1 *Question types*

4 Responding

Psychotherapist Carl Rogers (1902-1987) listed five types of responses in our daily conversations:

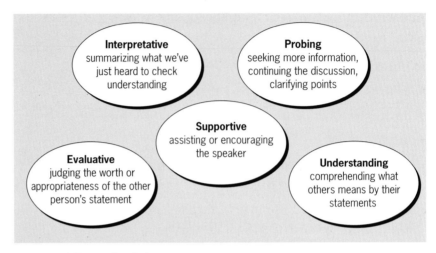

Figure 1.6 *Types of verbal response*

The key to using them is to choose a response for a specific situation. Many of us favour one or two types of response and use them inappropriately.

5 Feedback

Feedback is often associated with interviews or other processes by which we review performance. It is also used to check that messages have been received and understood and it is this context on which you will focus in this section. Shirley Taylor (2000) states that feedback is: '...the final stage of the communication process. Without it, the sender will not know if the communication process has been successful.'

Non-verbal communication

Various commentators agree that a message is made up of 7% words, 38% voice tonality and 55% body language!

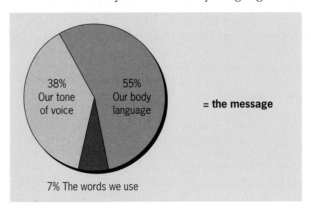

Figure 1.7 *The impact of verbal and non-verbal communication*

Source: Murdock and Scutt (2003)

Non-verbal communication is made up of the messages that we convey using our tone of voice, facial expressions, gestures and body language (e.g. posture) and increasingly emoticons like smiley faces. We may use these signals to strengthen our verbal message or, unwittingly, to diminish or contradict it. Similarly we can use other people's non-verbal signals to confirm their verbal message.

Guirdham (1995) lists the following non-verbal cues:

◆ Speech: rate, volume and pitch reveal emotions. For example, when we are angry or excited we speak more quickly, more loudly and at a higher pitch.

◆ Eye contact: people often avoid direct eye contact if they are uncomfortable with the person they are speaking to, or if they find the subject difficult or embarrassing.

◆ Facial expression: smiling, frowning, etc. reflect emotions and usually match the expression in the eyes.

◆ Posture: this may be receptive or defensive. When communication goes well, participants may 'mirror' each other's posture by, for example, leaning towards each other.

◆ Gestures: small movements such as finger tapping or fiddling with your hair may reveal feelings such as boredom or lack of confidence.

Murdock and Scutt (2003) extend this list to include the following:

◆ Proximity: our distance from other people can indicate our feelings towards them – though it is important to recognize that cultural influences can determine proximity.

◆ Appearance: we respond to people's appearance and dress. For example, within a business context we tend to associate smart clothes and good grooming with efficiency and effectiveness.

Emoticons help to extend the communication capabilities of different new media. Wikkipedia describes them as follows.

> Emoticons are a form of paralanguage commonly used as extended interpunction symbols in e-mail, instant messaging, online chat, bulletin boards and Internet forums; without them simple statements could be misinterpreted.

Source: http://en.wikipedia.org/wiki/Emoticon Accessed October 2006

The recognition that language and especially written language is easy to misinterpret is at the heart of the use and value of emoticons, pictures and icons in modern communications. Interpreting non-verbal signals can help us to understand what another person is feeling and thus read their words more accurately. It is not, however, an exact science. Individuals who are familiar with such signals may be adept at using them and thus be able to disguise their emotions more effectively than others.

Allan and Barbara Pease (2004) suggest three rules for accurately reading non-verbal signals:

Rule 1: Read gestures in clusters. Gestures, like words in a sentence, come in clusters and you need to put together at least three signals to 'read' what a person is thinking or feeling.

Rule 2: Look for congruence. Research suggests that non-verbal signals have much more impact than words and if the two are incongruent (i.e. don't correspond) people tend to rely on the non-verbal message and disregard the verbal content. It is important, therefore to look a match between gesture clusters and the words that are spoken. Sigmund Freud once reported that while a patient was verbally expressing happiness with her marriage, she was unconsciously slipping her wedding ring on and off her finger. Freud was aware of the significance of this unconscious gesture and was not surprised when marriage problems began to surface.

Source: Pease and Pease (2004)

Rule 3: Read gestures in context. If it's a windy day and a person is blinking a lot, they may be having trouble with their contact lenses rather than trying to lie to you! You should always factor in the circumstances in which communication is taking place before making any judgements about non-verbal signals.

Although we need to be wary of misinterpreting non-verbal cues, it is still useful to understand some of the most commonly used signals. This table summarises what each of the following signals suggests about how the person is feeling.

Non-verbal signal	Could indicate
Sitting back in a chair, legs crossed at the ankle	Relaxed, confident
Fidgeting with hands, drumming on the table, tapping feet	Nervous, anxious
Sitting with head down, mouth slightly down turned	Depressed, dejected
Sitting forward in a chair, maintaining eye contact	Interested
Palms open, shoulders raised, eyebrows raised	Submission, lack of aggression
Flaring nostrils, hands on hips, torso thrust forward from the hips	Defiance, aggression
Arms crossed and fists clenched	Hostility, defensiveness
Shoulders sagging, slumped posture, eyes looking downwards	Sadness, fear, weariness
Head lifted high, chin jutting forward	Superiority, fearlessness, arrogance

Table 1.2 *Interpreting non-verbal signals*

Cultural differences have a profound impact on non-verbal signals. If you are working with people in other countries, or in a multi-cultural environment, you should be guarded with your own signals and slow to jump to conclusions about other people's signals. Being culturally aware can prevent you from making serious mistakes.

> Pease and Pease (2004) cite the example of the signature gesture of the Texas Longhorn football team in which the index finger and little fingers are raised to represent the horns of the bull and the second and third fingers are bent into the palm and held down by the thumb. In Italy this gesture is known as the 'Cuckold' and is highly offensive. In 1985 five Americans were arrested in Rome for using this gesture outside the Vatican when they heard about a major Longhorn win back in the USA.

In whatever context we would all do well to follow the advice of Ezra Pound.

> Good writers are those who keep the language efficient. That is to say, keep it accurate, keep it clear.

Ezra Pound (1885–1972)

Activity 1
Transmit your message

Objective

This activity will help you to examine the transmission model in more detail and identify potential communication problems.

Task

As a manager, your communication skills are of paramount importance, particularly when directing or guiding your team members.

1. Identify an instruction that you communicated recently to a member (or members) of your team. Make a brief note of the content of your message.

2. Describe the way in which you encoded your message using words and non-verbal signals so that the receiver could understand it. For example, did you modify the language you used, employ specialist jargon, give detailed explanations? In retrospect, can you identify ways in which you could have improved your coding?

3. Next, think about the channel you used to communicate your message. Did you use the most appropriate medium? If you had to give the message again, would you choose a different channel?

4. Did your audience (the receiver) decode and understand your message? Make notes about how you checked their understanding.

5. Finally consider any problems that you experienced in delivering your message. How could you improve on your delivery?

1 The message

2 The code

3 The channel

4 The receiver

5 Problems and ways to improve

Feedback

In this activity you examined the transmission communication model in some detail. To communicate effectively, the code and channel that you choose will be influenced not only by the content of the message but also by the needs of the receiver. If you don't select appropriate words and non-verbal signals, your audience may well miss the point that you're trying to make. It is essential to include a mechanism for gaining feedback from the receiver so that you can measure understanding. This may be by simply asking, 'Is that clear?'

Barriers to communication

Are you ready to listen?

Total Eclipse of Communication
Author unknown

From: Managing Director
To: Executive Director

'Tomorrow morning there will be a total eclipse of the sun at nine o'clock. This is something which we cannot see every day. So let the work-force line up outside, in their best clothes to watch it. To mark the occasion of this rare occurrence, I will personally explain the phenomenon to them. If it is raining we will not be able to see it very well and in that case the work force should assemble in the canteen.'

From: Executive Director
To: Departmental Head

'By order of the Managing Director, there will be a total eclipse of the sun at nine o' clock tomorrow morning. If it is raining we will not be able to see it in our best clothes, on the site. In this case the disappearance of the sun will be followed through in the canteen. This is something we cannot see happening every day.'

From: Departmental Heads
To: Sectional Heads

'By order of the Managing Director, we shall follow the disappearance of the sun in our best clothes, in the canteen at nine o'clock tomorrow morning. The Managing Director will tell us whether it is going to rain. This is something which we cannot see happen every day.'

From: Section Heads
To: Foreman

'If it is raining in the canteen tomorrow morning, which is something that we cannot see happen every day, the Managing director in his best clothes, will disappear at nine o' clock.'

From: Foreman
To: All Operators

'Tomorrow morning at nine o' clock, the Managing Director will disappear. It's a pity that we can't see this happen every day.'

You will have come across miscommunications at work and in life. This example illustrates how people can distort the message according to what they want or think they should be hearing. During the communication process, our messages may be blocked or distorted. This can happen at various stages of the communication process: the sender may not code the message effectively, the medium may be inappropriate or affected by external factors such as noise, and the receiver may not have the knowledge or skill to decode the message. The problem often lies in attitudes, in other words in the way we deliver a message and the ability or willingness of our audience to receive it.

Edwin H. Friedman a leadership writer, described it like this.

The colossal misunderstanding of our time is the assumption that insight will work with people who are unmotivated to change. Communication does not depend on syntax, or eloquence, or rhetoric, or articulation but on the emotional context in which the message is being heard. People can only hear you when they are moving toward you, and they are not likely to when your words are pursuing them. Even the choicest words lose their power when they are used to overpower. Attitudes are the real figures of speech.

So does what we say matter, or is it just the 'emotional context' and the way in which we say it? Think about it. You are listening to a great speaker, but you have something else on your mind. It's very difficult to concentrate. The problem may be that your mind is rightly on something more important or it may be that the so called 'great speaker' hasn't grabbed your attention. A range of factors will come into play, but if people aren't ready to listen its unlikely that your message will get through.

Coding and decoding

Guirdham (1995) developed a model to illustrate other possible sources of error at each stage of the communication process.

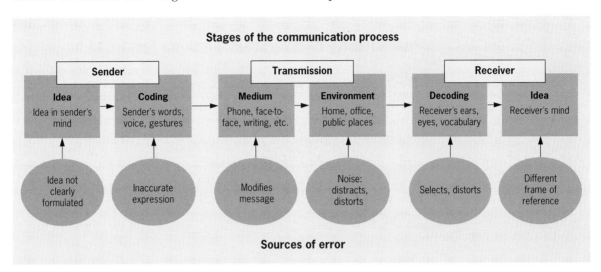

Figure 1.8 *Sources of error at each stage in the communication process*

This table shows some of the reasons why errors can occur in the communication process.

Stage	Why errors may occur
Sender: idea	Ideas may not be clearly formulated before coding and transmission begins. For example, you may want to dispute a decision but you haven't thought about alternative ways forward.
Sender: coding	You don't have the right vocabulary to express your thoughts. You use overly complex language or jargon that the receiver cannot understand.
Transmission: medium	The medium may modify the message. For example, if you communicate by telephone or in writing, the receiver cannot use your non-verbal signals to help interpret your message.
Transmission: environment	The environment can distort the message. For example, noise on a telephone line could distort a message. Things happening around the sender or receiver (e.g. other people speaking, coming into the room, etc.) may distract them from the message.
Receiver: decoding	Decoding may distort the message. The receiver may not hear the correct words, or may read written communications too quickly and misunderstand the message.
Receiver: idea	The receiver's perceptions may distort the message. For example, their beliefs or mindset based on previous experience may create a barrier so that they don't listen to the message.

Table 1.3 *Errors in the communication process*

In ongoing communication, as messages go backwards and forwards between sender and receiver, the potential for error increases. In group situations, such as meetings, where all the participants have differing perceptions, the scope for errors increases still further. It is not unusual for a group of people to come out of a meeting with very different ideas about what has been agreed.

One way to avoid or at least minimize these errors is to use feedback to check understanding. Continually check back, asking, 'Does that mean...?', 'So do we agree...?' 'Can we go back...?' to confirm that the message has been transmitted accurately.

Perceptions and context

Some sources of error are not tied to specific stages in the communication process. For example, both sender and receiver may have differing perceptions or make assumptions. It is therefore important to examine the following main types of barrier.

Environment

The environment in which the communication takes place may contain physical or emotional barriers.

Physical barriers include:

- interference – distractions, noise, problems with technology
- discomfort – circumstances which affect concentration such as being too hot or too cold, feeling ill, etc.

Emotional barriers, such as one person feeling angry or unhappy, can affect the atmosphere in a meeting and distort messages.

Language

Language is at the heart of the coding and decoding processes. Problems can arise if the language used is unfamiliar to one of the parties, for example:

> **If you talk to a man in a language he understands, that goes to his head. If you talk to him in his language, that goes to his heart.**
> **Nelson Mandela**

- Jargon: many professions rely heavily on jargon and have their own 'language' that is impenetrable to outsiders. Senders can use jargon as a form of power over those who are not 'in the loop'.
- Acronyms and abbreviations: although these can form an useful shorthand, they exclude receivers who are not familiar with their meaning.

A prime example of the problems that inappropriate language can raise is the use of 'text language' in transmitting both phone messages and emails. Although the message may be perfectly comprehensible to someone who texts regularly, it will be meaningless to others who haven't acquired this skill.

A second problem with language is that we assume words have the same meaning for different people. Our understanding of a word is influenced by our background knowledge, culture and experience.

Culture

Culture can impact on the interpretation of non-verbal signals. Pease and Pease (2004) identify a range of noticeable cultural differences in the ways that people:

◆ greet each other. For example, some cultures kiss while other are satisfied with the briefest of handshakes

◆ use gestures: a potential minefield since even the most seemingly innocuous gesture (to the British!) such as pointing with the forefinger can be offensive to some Asian cultures

◆ use personal space: in general, northern Europeans and Americans are less comfortable with touching than southern Europeans, Indians and people from the Middle East.

Guirdham (1995) says that to work successfully with people of other cultures, you must understand their ways of working. For example, Americans value direct verbal interaction and 'straight speaking' whereas the Japanese value spiral logic and indirect verbal interaction. Both the Japanese and Chinese place great importance on 'saving face' and ensuring that neither the sender nor receiver of a message is embarrassed. Consequently they may appear to understand a message when they don't, or to agree with you when they have no intention of complying with your wishes.

Perceptions

The term 'perceptions' encompasses a range of thought processes, including the assumptions we make, and our subconscious attitudes that inform our values and beliefs. Differing perceptions can form major barriers in communication. Because perceptions are often 'invisible' and subconscious they frequently go undetected. In some cases perceptions are used to manipulate people's thinking. Our perceptions are influenced by the following.

1 **Jumping to conclusions**
   A father and his son were driving to a football game when their car stalled on the railway tracks. In the distance a train blew a warning. Frantically the father tried to start the engine, but in his panic he couldn't turn the key. When the train hit the car the father was killed outright. The son was rushed to hospital, needing immediate surgery. As he was wheeled into the operating theatre, the surgeon blanched and muttered 'I can't operate on this boy – he's my son'.

   It's common for people to take a couple of minutes to get the real answer to this riddle. Is the surgeon the boy's real father? Is it someone else's father in the car? In reality the surgeon is the boy's mother.

   One of the characteristics of perceptions concerns our need to make sense of our environment and to search for meaning. We use our experience to fill in the gaps in incomplete data. Although this is useful, it can also lead us to jump to conclusions which can be wildy inaccurate. Think about times when you and a colleague have drawn two very different conclusions from a situation. Why was that?

2   **Unstated assumptions about the other person's beliefs and intentions**

> Our assumptions are your windows on the world. Scrub them off every once and a while, or the light won't come in.

Alan Alda, actor

3   **Stereotyping**
    Think for a moment about your own stereotypes and how they might affect the way that you communicate, either as sender or receiver of a message by completing the following sentences with three terms that you think most accurately describe each group:

    Religious leaders are...
    Teachers are...
    Artists are...
    Engineers are...

    Lipmann (1922) describes stereotypes as pictures in the head. He claims that when we meet a teacher or an artist, or someone who fits our stereotype, we assign them personality traits based on the picture and make assumptions about what and how that person thinks.

4   **Assuming that the audience has the knowledge or capacity to understand the message**

5   **Perceived status particularly if we think that the person we're communicating with is of much higher or lower status than we are**

6   **Values and beliefs**

The organisation

The organisation or group in which we operate can be a barrier to communication because of a:

◆   lack of appropriate communication channels. For example, you know that someone in the organization has the information you need but you don't know who they are

◆   culture that discourages informal communication by insisting on putting everything in writing

◆   culture of individualism that makes it difficult to obtain a corporate view

◆   culture that discourages individual expression

◆   culture of conflict that leads to information being distorted or withheld.

It would be impossible to overcome all these barriers: human beings are simply not perfect enough to put their thoughts into words without sometimes distorting them. We can, however, reduce the risk of miscommunication by taking some simple steps.

◆ Be clear in your own mind about what you want to communicate.

◆ Select the right medium and use it appropriately.

◆ Step into the receiver's shoes and anticipate the impact of your communication.

◆ Use feedback to encourage two-way communication and check understanding.

◆ When possible, communicate directly, face-to-face so that you can use non-verbal signals.

◆ Limit the number of links in the communication chain.

The last point is particularly important within the context of organisational communications. Try to avoid messages being diffused through various levels of management; they may well get distorted as they move downwards or upwards.

Activity 2
Overcome communication barriers

In this activity you will focus on identifying and overcoming barriers that you've experienced in verbal communication.

1 Think about a conversation you have had recently with an individual or group of people that didn't go as well as you wanted it to. You should have been sending the message. For example, you may have been discussing a colleague's performance with them or delivering instructions.

Here is an example:

Communication I was involved in:	Communication channel
Informing team about new efficiency targets that will be rolled out over the next three months	Presentation to group of six team members

Communication I was involved in:	Communication channel

2 Reflect on the communication and identify the barriers that may have led to distortion. Use the headings in the table to list these barriers and suggest possible ways of overcoming them.

Type of barrier	Sender	Transmission	Receiver
Environment			
Barrier			
Solution			
Language			
Barrier			
Solution			
Culture			
Barrier			
Solution			

Perception

Barrier

Solution

The organisation

Barrier

Solution

Other

Barrier

Solution

Feedback

The number of barriers you identified may have surprised you. It is relatively straightforward to eliminate environmental barriers by choosing the appropriate time and place for the communication. For example, don't try to have a complex or confidential discussion in a busy corridor or place an order down a crackling phone line.

Eliminating 'sender' barriers means thinking though the message in your own mind first. It also means communicating assertively and making sure you choose the appropriate medium. For example, give complex instructions in writing rather than expect people to remember them, use appropriate language that your receiver will understand. Minimising 'receiver' barriers from your end involves getting to know the receiver – their attitudes and beliefs – so you can see things from their point of view.

Connections

Connections, such as one-to-one, one-to-many and many-to-many, can be achieved in any number of ways from the traditional report to instant messaging, texts, teleconferencing, video links, intranet broadcasting, pod casting and blogs. The opportunities are endless. Here are two examples about e-government and virtual team working. How well do they work?

> Government is more accessible than ever thanks to the web, kiosks, digital TV and call centres. The challenge now is to persuade people to ditch traditional methods of communication and embrace e-channels. Studies have been conducted into the potential benefits of e-government and the benefits include more direct contact with the people who run the country, simple systems to take advantage of your democratic rights, quicker services and cheaper services. But it all takes time. In the meantime services need to be provided for all comers and this means a multichannel approach. A survey carried out by the e-Citizen national project, reported in the Guardian newspaper concluded that:
>
> One piece of good news is that Britons seem to like the idea of being e-citizens. Few, however, have tried it.

Source: http://politics.guardian.co.uk/egovernment/story/
0,,1422958,00.html

Virtual working may increasingly be the way more of us work in the future. The following text highlights the difficulties faced by many people in organisations who are working with people they never or rarely see. How does this impact on the way they work and interact?

> A study by Cisco Systems shows that virtual teams can take up to four times as long to build trust than face-to-face teams. If you throw different cultures into the mix, it can take those virtual teams up to 17 weeks before they bond and perform as well as a team based in one location.
>
> 'Virtual communication is on the increase,' says Caroline Shearsmith, occupational psychologist at Pearn Kandola who carried out the study. 'At the same time, there is resistance against virtual teams, who struggle to develop trust because the virtual communication is depersonalised.'
>
> The study, called The Psychology of Effective Business Communications in Geographically Dispersed Teams, comes on the heels of a 2005 Economist Intelligence Unit survey of retailing and consumer goods companies. The survey found that the second most important factor for improving productivity

over the next 15 years - after more efficient organisational structures - was better communication among the workforce.

Source: Kate Bulkley September 28, 2006
The Guardian http://technology.guardian.co.uk/online/insideit/story/
0,,1882176,00.html

The conclusion of both of these studies was that a mix of communications media would help bring people together including visual media like video conferencing for teams and texting or messaging for e-government.

Is technology changing our brains?

This is the interesting question posed by Susan Greenfield in the House of Lords in April 2006.

She examines the way we communicate and Jackie Ashley, former MP, highlights the following points in an article in the Guardian.

In just a couple of decades, we have slipped away from a culture based essentially on words to one based essentially on images, or pictures. This is probably one of the great shifts in the story of modern humans, but we take it almost for granted.

Susan Greenfield goes on to describe traditional education and learning through books:

She begins by analysing the process of traditional book-reading, which involves following an author through a series of interconnected steps in a logical fashion. We read other narratives and compare them, and so 'build up a conceptual framework that enables us to evaluate further journeys... One might argue that this is the basis of education ... It is the building up of a personalised conceptual framework, where we can relate incoming information to what we know already. We can place an isolated fact in a context that gives it significance.' Traditional education, she says, enables us to 'turn information into knowledge.'

Jackie Ashley MP summarises her worries like this.

The flickering up and flashing away again of multimedia images do not allow those connections, and therefore the context, to build up. Instant yuk or wow factors take over. Memory, once built up in a verbal and reading culture, matters less when everything can be summoned at the touch of a button (or, soon,

> with voice recognition, by merely speaking). In a short attention-span world, fed with pictures, the habit of contemplation and the patient acquisition of knowledge are in retreat.

It's an area for further investigation. But there are others with different views.

Mark Prensky in *Digital Game Based Learning* describes young people as 'digital natives'. They are the Nintendo and MTV generation who:

> process information more rapidly than ever before, prefer graphic to text, and work on several fronts at once, making them champion multitaskers. As a result today's new workforce is eager for new challenges.

Mark Prensky (2001)

Whatever the truth is, it is evident that we need to change and consider the channels we use to communicate more effectively and more fully and in doing so we may need our brains to evolve.

Over connected?

Many organisations adopted technology with gusto and equipped their employees with a range of technology to help them keep in touch. It remains a good idea in principle, especially if it helps to reduce travelling to meetings, to the office or between offices. However as we have seen before we are not 'creatures of logic', but 'creatures of emotion'. So what could go wrong? Do we use too much technology?

The technology takes over – people too often neglect to think about their audience, their message and what really needs to be said and use the functions of the technology to get them through. How many long PowerPoint presentations have you sat through?

We rely on the technology too much – have you ever sent an email when a conversation might have been better, quicker and more effective or replied using 'reply to all' when plainly half of the people didn't really need to know?

Technology has a bit of a 'big brother' effect – which we naturally rebel against. It gets a bit much when people can find out when you are at your desk through the instant messaging system.

We begin to resent the intrusion of technology from work into our private lives. People are increasingly taking their work on holiday with them in the form of a Blackberry or mobile phone with internet connection.

There are then problems with connectedness, but it would be difficult to imagine life now without most of our means of communication. Perhaps the answer is that we need to get better at managing them, so that the communication media doesn't manage us.

Organisational communications

The conclusion, in the digital world seems to be that multichannel approaches to intra and inter organisational communications are here to stay. Channels need to be carefully chosen to match the purpose and the audience. If you are talking to well 'connected' young people – the 'digital natives', your choice of media may be more flexible, electronic and fast. They are a group for whom, however, personal contact may hold great significance. Use it wisely for the important and personal messages. Other audiences still prefer personal contact above anything else. There is nothing, and probably never will be anything to replace a face-to-face meeting with a new client or a personal service delivered to the door.

Within many organisations you will find a hierarchy of media-use with face-to-face at the the top. Email is a workhorse in the middle and noticeboards and intranets are seen as repositories for useful information to support knowledge management, but not a means of communicating important and urgent messages. To determine your media you will need to think about how different parts of the organisation communicate with each other, how information is transmitted (sending, coding, receiving and decoding) who you are communicating with (what their preferences for communication styles are), what the message is and how important it is, transactional analysis and perceptions of the sender and receiver and how knowledge is managed so that we can store and dispose of it. The essence is to match the channel to the audience and the message.

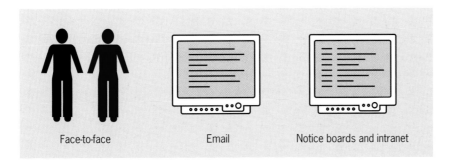

Face-to-face   Email   Notice boards and intranet

Figure 1.9 *Matching the channels to the audience*

In recent years, changes in organisations have impacted on how communication takes place.

◆ We now accept that people, rather than processes, are the lifeblood of organisations. Without effective communications, people cannot be managed to achieve results so a greater emphasis is paced on developing communications skills and procedures.

- The tendency towards flatter, less hierarchical organisations has, in many companies, encouraged less formality and more open communication systems.

- The move towards team working and project management encourages greater collaborative skills.

- The trend towards out-sourcing has led to new patterns of communication with suppliers and customers.

- New media (particularly electronic media) has made communication faster and more direct.

- Improved global communications mean that virtual teams are possible. They mean that people may be working in different time zones, with different languages and across vast distances, but they will be working on the same project.

When Hewlett-Packard's executive committee decided in June to ask all employees to take a voluntary payroll reduction, the decision was posted immediately on the company's @HP portal, the intranet that binds together nearly 90,000 employees in 150 countries. A tool enabling employees to volunteer for the reduction accompanied the announcement. The first day 10,000 employees signed up; within three days 30,000 had volunteered. Kathy Dolan, director of @HP, believes the portal played a central role in making the program work. Instead of finding out by word of mouth whether people were signing up, employees could check the site to find the current tally of volunteers; as the count steadily increased, it convinced more people to participate. Ultimately, more than 90 percent of HP's employees volunteered for pay cuts.

Source: www.darwinmag.com/read/110101/intranet.html

Shared or collaborative working

The digital age has also brought new ways of working which have revolutionised customer/supplier relationships, which are opening up channels for skills sharing between organisations and which attempt to capitalise on the knowledge and information stored, but often languishing, within an organisation. Collaborative working attempts to break down the barriers of communication and share knowledge more widely. It is a bold move, especially for organisations and individuals who see knowledge as power.

Sharing data and information is a vital component of a true collaborative relationship, enabling:

- those collaborating to add value to data and information by sharing their insights and ideas, discussing options, and raising questions

- members of the team to share activities and actions, and track progress
- people to organise and search for information more effectively and efficiently.

An effective collaborative working environment tends to:

- integrate processes
- share tacit knowledge and personal insights
- generate new and better ideas
- use joint problem-solving
- use joint risk identification
- learn faster.

As a manager, one of your key roles is to facilitate communication, not only within your department but also across the organisation and between organisations. The bottom line is that communication is no longer a 'soft' skill. It drives individual, organisational and inter organisational performance and if it's going in a new direction you'll need to be open to the possibilities.

Activity 3
Your contribution to the information flow in your organisation

Objective

To analyse the way in which you contribute to the flow of information in your organisation.

Task

Ideally information flows around your organisation and is passed freely from senior management through to the most junior of staff – and vice versa.

Describe how information is passed downwards in your organisation from senior management to staff. What mechanisms are used?

In your management role, how do you contribute to this process?

How is information passed across the organisation, i.e. from department to department and from manager to manager?

In your management role, how do you contribute to this process?

How is information passed upwards, so that senior managers understand what staff are thinking and experiencing?

In your management role, how do you contribute to this process?

Feedback

Hopefully your notes will illustrate a more integrated system where information flows easily downwards, upwards, and horizontally, from department to department. Consider what the potential is for more knowledge and information sharing in the structures that exist, and how the structures could change to facilitate a more collaborative approach.

Your role is particularly important because you act as the intermediary between senior management (who are often the decision-takers) and where decisions have to be interpreted and implemented. This is not always an easy role to fulfil and you may have identified situations where the information flow is impeded or non-existent. In such cases, think of possible solutions such as:

1. regular discussion sessions in which team members are encouraged to talk openly with you. These will be 'off the record' rather than related to a formal reporting system

2. informal meetings with managers at your level so that you can compare your experiences and highlight areas of concern

3. open communication between senior managers and staff lower down the hierarchy through forums or using the organisation's Intranet. Again, the emphasis is on encouraging openness – individuals must feel that they can speak their mind without any comeback.

Don't forget that an information flow should also allow for other stakeholders (customers, suppliers, shareholders, etc.) to contribute and for their messages to be heard.

◆ Recap

Explore basic concepts and theories of communication

◆ Communication is a process that involves words and non-verbal signals, a sender, receiver and medium of transmission.

◆ Communication problems can arise if the sender chooses an inappropriate code or medium for the message and the receiver cannot decode it.

Explore how communication is made up of verbal and non-verbal elements

◆ We communicate verbally, non-verbally, formally and informally. We adapt our language and mannerisms according to the circumstances in which we are communicating.

◆ Verbal communication involves active listening, reflecting and summarising, questioning, responding, and giving and receiving feedback.

◆ Non-verbal communication is made up of the messages we convey using tone of voice, facial expressions, gestures and body language.

Assess the factors that commonly create barriers to effective communication

◆ The main barriers include environment, language, culture, perception.

◆ Barriers can be overcome by paying attetion to the context of communication, selecting the right medium and by trying to see things the way the receiver does.

Examine how communication takes place in your organisation

◆ As well as understanding the principles of interpersonal communication, managers need to consider how communication takes place within the organisation, how information is transmitted and knowledge is managed.

◆ Ideally information and knowledge will flow upwards and downwards and horizontally across the organisation.

▶▶ More @

Guirdham, M. (1995) *Interpersonal Skills at Work*, Prentice Hall
Providing systematic coverage of all aspects of dealing with people face-to-face, this text demonstrates how basic skills can be applied to work activities and situations.

Pease, A. and Pease, B. (2004) *The Definitive Book of Body Language*, Orion
This authoritative guide, written with great humour and insight, reveals all the secrets of body language to give you more confidence and control in any situation.

Taylor, S. (2000) *Essential Communication Skills*, Longman
Subtitled The Ultimate Guide to Business Communications, this is a comprehensive textbook and reference guide on the essentials of both written and oral communication skills

Dixon, R. (2003) *The Management Task*, Butterworth Heinemann
Rob Dixon addresses the task of management in terms of the different processes involved, eg. planning, decision-making, communication, and the more specific management functions such as personnel, marketing, and the environment of management and business.

Two excellent websites providing resources on communication and many other management skills:

www.mindtools.com

www.businessballs.com

2   Meetings

How many meetings have you taken part in during the last two weeks – and how did you feel about them? Did they help you do your job better or do you feel that you could have spent the time more productively? Were they face-to-face or computer/telephone mediated?

Carefully planned meetings that are convened for a clear purpose can save time, improve motivation and solve problems. By bringing people together and giving them a chance to exchange information and opinions, they foster a team spirit that cannot be achieved through less direct communication methods such as the intranet, letter or email.

> 'For lots of people, meetings (meetings, and more meetings) are politics at its worst, and an epic waste… But the point many miss is that meetings really aren't about doing things. They are about figuring out the way so-and-so is thinking, and feeling, paving the way for an initiative that is months off, edging towards some eventual consensus about this and that.

Tom Peters, article in The Independent on Sunday, 1995, quoted in *The Hutchinson Dictionary of Business Quotations* (1996)

Unfortunately, many of us sit through badly planned meetings where we feel we are wasting time. Guy Browning sums up this view.

> Half of every working day is spent in meetings, half of which are not worth having, and of those that are, half the time is wasted. Which means that nearly one third of office life is spent in small rooms with people you don't like, doing things that don't matter.

Guy Browning, October 2006

The Guardian http://money.guardian.co.uk/work/story/0,,1924889,00.html

This section examines the purpose of meetings and suggests ways in which you, as a participant or leader, can get the most out of them.

In this section you will:

◆ consider the value and limitations of meetings as a means of exchanging information and making decisions

◆ prepare to participate in meetings and use your speaking and listening skills to contribute effectively

◆ prepare to lead a meeting and follow up afterwards.

Why do we need a meeting?

You are probably involved in many different types of meeting including:

♦ impromptu meetings with colleagues and team members to resolve an immediate problem

♦ informal, but scheduled, meetings such as team briefings, meetings with clients and project meetings

♦ formal meetings such as board and committee meetings.

Caunt (2000) suggests that the main purposes of meetings are to:

♦ impart information

♦ elicit views

♦ stimulate new ideas

♦ motivate a team

♦ reach decisions.

Fleming (1997) suggests that meetings have many benefits. Meeting face-to-face can help people get to know each other, help them draw from a variety of experiences, improve decision making and build the team. Despite these potential benefits, many of them fail to deliver a satisfactory outcome. Hodgson and Hodgson (1993) identify six reasons why meetings fail to achieve their objectives:

♦ **Failure of preparation**: participants were inadequately briefed or didn't bother to prepare. 'Fail to prepare and prepare to fail'.

♦ **Failure of purpose**: this could be because the meeting wasn't held for a valid reason but was the product of habit – 'We always have a meeting first thing on Monday morning'. Alternatively the purpose of the meeting may not have been communicated to the participants; for example, they expect a brief review but are subjected to a detailed presentation so haven't put aside enough time and become increasingly impatient.

♦ **Failure of communication** before, during or after the meeting.

♦ **Failure of resource utilization**, when experts are brought into a meeting but don't make a useful contribution.

♦ **Failure of decision**: meetings sometimes end after long discussion without a clear decision being made. Decision making can be impeded if participants have hidden agendas which they are determined to promote, if they fail to appreciate the reality of the situation they're dealing with, or if participants lack the courage to make difficult decisions.

♦ **Failure of implementation**: participants may be fired up with enthusiasm when they leave a meeting but that enthusiasm must be transmitted into action afterwards.

Meetings are also expensive. Try this simple calculation. Divide your salary by 200 (the number of working days in a year), then by 8 (the number of hours in the working day) and make a note of your 'hourly rate'. Multiply that by the number of hours you spent in meetings during the last week. Add the 'hourly rates' of the other participants, plus travelling costs, room and facilities hire, preparation time, etc. and you'll get an idea of what meetings cost your organisation.

It makes sense, therefore, to consider other communication methods before you call a meeting. Could the same objectives be achieved by:

◆ telephone calls

◆ a video conference

◆ written communications (letter, phone, fax, email)

◆ a briefing note

◆ an informal chat with individuals?

If you always have a meeting with certain people at a set time every week or month, it's worth considering whether it really has an objective. Could you do away with the meeting altogether or just change the format?

Activity 4
Analyse meetings and investigate alternative communication methods

Objective

This activity asks you to consider the various types of meeting in which you are involved, consider whether they are essential and if you could use other communication methods.

Task

1. Think about four meetings that you have participated in during the last two weeks. In column 1 of this grid, describe the type of meeting (e.g. informal, formal, impromptu, etc.).

2. In column 2, outline its purpose (it may have had more than one).

3. In column 3, make a note of whether this purpose was achieved. If it wasn't, briefly describe the reasons why it failed to meet its objectives.

4. In column 4, suggest alternative communication methods that might have achieved the objectives successfully.

	Type	Purpose	Were the objectives of the meeting achieved?	Alternative communication method
Meeting 1				
Meeting 2				
Meeting 3				
Meeting 4				

Feedback

For many managers, meetings comprise more than 60% of their working day, and they lose track of the number and type they participate in. You may have been surprised at the range of meetings you attend.

Essentially meetings are groups of people and research shows that groups work best when their purpose is clear and there are agreed working practices. If you work in an organisation where meetings are tightly structured and only ever held for a clearly defined purpose, then you may have answered 'yes' in every box in column 3. Unfortunately most of us are not so lucky and will have identified meetings that failed to achieve a positive outcome.

Obviously, in some circumstances a meeting will be essential so you may have left some of the boxes in column 4 blank. You may, however, have identified alternative communication methods for other meetings, such as informal discussion or correspondence that would have saved time and money.

Attending meetings

Preparation

As with any business task, you need to prepare before you take action. Preparation for a meeting falls into three categories.

◆ The preparations you'll make if you are organising the meeting.

◆ The preparations you'll make if you are participating in a meeting.

◆ The preparations you'll make if you are leading a meeting.

The person who convenes the meeting will determine its objectives but they may delegate the responsibility for organising it to somebody else. If that 'somebody else' is you, start planning by using the 4 Ws.

1. *What is the meeting about?* Define its purpose and consider whether it is really necessary. What outcome do you want from the meeting?

2. *Who will attend?* Make a list of the people who'll be there and identify their purpose (i.e. make a note of who will take the minutes, who will give presentations, who will chair, etc.) How will you inform these people about the meeting?

3. *When will the meeting take place?* Does it need to be at a specific time or could it be run asynchronously? Is the time suitable for most people to attend? Can they get to the venue before the start or have access to appropriate technology? When will you tell participants that the meeting is going to take place? Remember that timing can influence attendance. If a meeting is held early in the morning the participants may be fresher and more willing to deal with complex issues. If it's held after lunch you may find that participants are more tired, less alert, and less willing to contribute.

4. *Where will the meeting be held – online or face-to-face?* Is the venue big enough and accessible for everyone? Are the facilities (lighting, heating, air-conditioning, technology) adequate? Do you have plenty of tables and chairs and refreshments? Have you provided aids for the speakers such as flipcharts, PowerPoint hardware, video, etc.?

Preparing an agenda

'The agenda is the backbone of a meeting. Without an agenda, a meeting is far less likely to achieve its required outcome. The agenda acts as a control device which establishes the parameters of the meeting, assigns tasks, establishes order and sequence, and provides guidelines for timing.'

Source: Hodgson and Hodgson (1992)

If you wish to converse with me, define your terms Voltaire, French Philosopher and Writer

Because the agenda goes out before the meeting, it helps people to focus on what they have to do before, during and after the proceedings. The more informative the agenda, the more likely it is that people will be prepared to make effective contributions.

There are specific stages during the course of a formal meeting, and the order of these is dictated by the agenda. As a minimum, it should set out the following.

◆ Apologies for absence.

◆ Minutes of previous meetings.

◆ Matters arising from previous meetings.

◆ List of new items. Include the required outcome (e.g. 'decision on', 'review of', etc.), the name of the person who will speak and the approximate time for each item.

◆ Any other business.

◆ Date and time of next meeting.

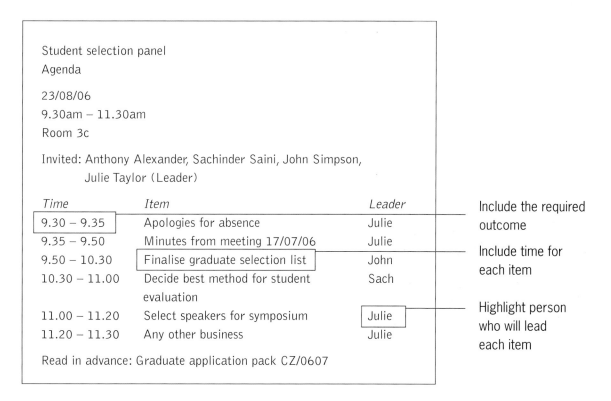

Student selection panel
Agenda

23/08/06
9.30am – 11.30am
Room 3c

Invited: Anthony Alexander, Sachinder Saini, John Simpson,
     Julie Taylor (Leader)

Time	Item	Leader
9.30 – 9.35	Apologies for absence	Julie
9.35 – 9.50	Minutes from meeting 17/07/06	Julie
9.50 – 10.30	Finalise graduate selection list	John
10.30 – 11.00	Decide best method for student evaluation	Sach
11.00 – 11.20	Select speakers for symposium	Julie
11.20 – 11.30	Any other business	Julie

Read in advance: Graduate application pack CZ/0607

Include the required outcome

Include time for each item

Highlight person who will lead each item

Figure 2.1 *Sample agenda*

If the meeting is less formal it's still worth knowing what you want to achieve, and who is going to take part. Encourage participants to suggest issues that they want to include. This will help you to identify important issues in advance and avoid too many side topics being raised.

How do you then decide the order of discussion? Obviously it would seem logical to put them in order of urgency and importance. Bear in mind, however, that matters early in the agenda tend to receive more discussion than those lower down the list. Towards the end of a meeting, people will make decisions more quickly because they are tired or have other business to attend to. It is not unknown for meeting organisers to slip contentious issues into the latter half of the agenda in the hope that they'll be dealt with quickly and controversy will be avoided!

Recording the meeting

Meetings can be recorded formally or informally. Think about the nature of your discussion. A brainstorming session wouldn't require minutes. Think about how the notes will be compiled and what means you can use to distribute them. Many people take notes directly on to computer devices and simply email them to participants later. The key thing is to know what is agreed and what actions need to be taken by whom.

More fomal meetings require a more formal process of sign off. Hodgson and Hodgson (1992) point out that some meetings such as company Annual General Meetings and Board Meetings are required by law to maintain written records of proceedings. This ensures that there is no argument in the future about what happened, there is a record of who is responsible for specific follow-up actions, and people who didn't attend can keep up to speed.

Unless you take shorthand very efficiently, your record of the meeting will be restricted to noting:

◆ facts

◆ decisions

◆ follow-up action that is required.

Although you won't be able to take down the proceedings verbatim, you should aim for accuracy. Try to transcribe your notes as quickly as possible after the meeting when the proceedings are still fresh in your mind.

Hodgson and Hodgson (1992) suggest that the minutes should contain the following information:

◆ Heading – title, date, time of meeting

◆ Names of people present. In a very formal meeting, you may include people who attend but do not participate until Any Other Business, such as members of the public, shareholders, etc.

◆ Apologies for absence

◆ Numbered agenda

◆ Suggestions and proposals, and who made them

◆ Decisions that are taken

◆ Actions that are agreed, the name of the person who is responsible for this and the date by which it will be completed

◆ Date of next meeting.

Everyone who was at the meeting should get a copy of the minutes so that they can read them before the next meeting. At the next meeting, the leader of the meeting will ask if they are an accurate record and sign them.

Preparing to participate in a meeting

If you are adequately prepared before you take part in a meeting, you will feel more confident about any contribution that you make. First get the mindset right. A meeting isn't something that's done 'to' people. It should be an opportunity for you and your team / customer/ stakeholder / manager to discuss issues and agree a way forward. Therefore start by thinking of the questions which you can ask to get the perspective of on the issue – what do you need to know. For example and depending on the meeting, by using questions such as:

◆ What is going well?

◆ What issues do you have?

◆ What has been particularly challenging? How did you overcome it?

Guirdham (1995) suggests that you need to prepare both your own information and views, and anticipate the position and views of other participants.

To prepare, you should:

- read the minutes or notes of the previous meeting
- read through the agenda and make a note of any areas where you have specific input
- collect relevant factual information
- think through issues before the meeting and consider your opinions
- assess who will be taking part and what they know about the situation, the issues etc
- identify possible areas of contention and consider how you will deal with these
- you may find it useful to talk to participants before the meeting to exchange information, determine their opinions and canvass support.

Source: adapted from Hindle (1998)

You may have been asked to provide particular input to a meeting or to make a formal presentation. For example, you may be giving a progress or feasibility report, or providing expert evidence or information to other participants. Hodgson and Hodgson (1992) give the following guidelines:

Prioritise. You may not have chance to say everything you want to so before the meeting decide what points are really important.

Keep your contribution short and to the point. You may find the topic fascinating, but others may be less interested so don't test their attention span.

Anticipate other people's questions and reactions and ensure that you have collected the information to address these.

Ask for questions and reactions. Some people prefer to respond to all questions at the end of their contribution but you may find it more useful to pick up on points as you go along. In this way you can check your audience's understanding.

Use examples to illustrate and enliven your argument.

Use visual aids. These include presentation techniques such as PowerPoint, as well as prompt notes for yourself and handouts for audience if they will be useful.

Communicating effectively in meetings

You will already be familiar with many of the techniques you can use to attract and maintain other people's attention during meetings, but it is useful to summarise them here.

To help illustrate these points:

- ◆ Signal your intentions as you speak. Tell people what you are doing by stating: 'I'd like to ask a question…', 'I want to raise a point about…'. This will get the attention of others in the meeting and focus them on you before you make a salient point.

- ◆ Ask questions both to check your own understanding of what other people are saying and to check that people understand you. As with any form of communication, accurate feedback is essential.

- ◆ Don't get personal. Focus on the issues that are under discussion and avoid being drawn into personal comment. However much antipathy you may feel for some of your colleagues, this is not the time to display it. Show them the same respect that you want to receive and let them have their say without interrupting.

- ◆ Use your voice and your body to gain and retain attention. The space is yours, and make your contribution active.

- ◆ Keep an open mind. You won't always get your own way in meetings so listen to what other have to say and be prepared to compromise.

- ◆ Props and pictures contribute a lot to any meeting. Remember this is a graphically rich age.

- ◆ Make eye contact with as many people in the room as possible – try to avoid excluding individuals.

- ◆ Look for and respond to non-verbal signals when people are listening to you. If they are fidgeting, looking out of the window or on the point of falling asleep, it is time to stop.

- ◆ Summarise key points at the end of your contribution and suggest a way forward.

- ◆ Remember that it is the leader's role to decide who speaks when and for how long. Ask the leader's permission to speak rather than interrupting.

Being seen and heard

In Managing Meetings, Hindle (1998) emphasises that you need to look and sound the part in order to get your message across. This includes making sure that you speak confidently. Confidence building is a circular process. If you appear to be confident people will perceive you as such and are more likely to be convinced by your arguments. You might remember from earlier that in any verbal communication your tone of voice and your body language have a great deal more impact than the words you use.

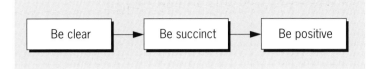

Figure 2.2 *Participating strongly*   Source: Hindle (1998)

Activity 5
Encourage participation in meetings

Objective

This activity will help you to support the contribution of others in meetings.

Task

If organising meetings is not one of your usual responsibilities, arrange with colleagues to take over the planning and preparation for a forthcoming meeting. Use this checklist to facilitate your planning.

What are the purpose and
aims of the meeting?

What outcomes do you want?

Who will attend?

When will the meeting
take place?

What time will it start
and finish?

How and when will you
inform participants
about the meeting?

Where will the meeting
take place?

☐ Is the venue accessible to all including those with disabilities?

☐ Have you booked the room and made sure you will not be interrupted?

How many chairs/tables do
you need?

Have you checked all facilities are in working order?   ☐ lighting
☐ heating
☐ ventilation

What audio-visual equipment will you need and have you checked this is in
working order?
☐
☐
☐

☐ Have you provided writing materials and for participants?

☐ Have you prepared duplicate copies of the agenda, briefing notes, etc.

☐ Have you provided refreshments for participants during the meeting?

☐ Has hospitality been arranged for after the meeting (e.g. coffee, lunch)?

Next you need to prepare an agenda for the meeting.

Remember to:

◆ invite participants to submit items

◆ include minutes from a previous meeting

◆ identify and list matters arising from the previous meeting

◆ order items in a logical way.

Your agenda

Feedback

The checklist will help you to organise the mechanics of a meeting. The more prepared you are, the less likely you are to experience delays and interruptions that will distract participants from the matters in hand.

Look at the presentation of your agenda and ensure that headings are clear. Compare your version with other agendas for formal meetings that have been circulated in your organisation. Send the agenda out at least one week before the meeting. You may want to check with participants that if they want to include any further issues.

It's important to set out an agenda for *all* meetings so that the proceedings have firm direction. For impromptu meetings or briefings, however, you could agree the agenda either verbally or in writing at the start of the meeting.

If you are organising a meeting, you will also be responsible for:

◆ making sure that accurate notes of the proceedings are taken so that the minutes can be prepared. You may want to minute the meeting yourself or delegate this task to someone else

◆ circulate an action plan after the meeting to make sure that people know how they are supposed to follow up.

Leading meetings

The leader of a meeting often determines the success – or failure in achieving its objectives. The Open University (1990) identifies two leading roles:

1. The traditional chairing role

Ensuring that business is completed by:

◆ ensuring fair play

◆ staying in charge

◆ remaining neutral.

2. The facilitative role

Helping the group to carry out its task by:

◆ clarifying goals

◆ encouraging participation

◆ looking for areas of agreement.

The balance of these roles may change depending on whether it is a formal meeting in which the traditional role will dominate, or an informal meeting in which the leader is more of a facilitator for open discussion. The role may also change as the person moves from the traditional to facilitative roles to allow for discussion in the middle of the meetings, then reverts to the more formal role to close it.

Hodgson and Hodgson (1992) point out that the leader should have a clear idea of the success criteria for the meeting so that they can achieve the best possible outcome.

> 'Some meetings are easy in that everyone knows what will be a 'good' result. But there are more difficult meetings when different people or power groups want different outcomes, which will require you to weigh up priorities. Even more difficult are meetings where different groups want opposing or contradictory outcomes. Here, you may need to spend some time negotiating success criteria before you can begin the meeting proper.'

Source: Hodgson and Hodgson (1992)

In a case like this, your first task will be to make the participants accept that they must 'agree to disagree' and to determine possible compromises that could be achieved during the course of the meeting.

This table summarises the leader's responsibilities and tasks.

Before the meeting	Prepare the agenda, organise venue, etc. if these are not being taken care of by a meeting organiser.
	Study agenda items, read previous meeting, anticipate difficult items.
	Look at the list of participants and identify who will need to be encouraged to contribute and who you will need to keep under control. Anticipate possible conflicts of interest.
During the meeting	Welcome participants, give an opening address that summarises developments to date and states the aims of the meeting.
	Keep to the timings of the agenda items and move the group on if they spend too long discussing one item.
	For items where you have a direct interest, delegate leadership to another participant.
	Introduce an item, explain what is to be discussed, time available and the required outcome.
	Listen more than you talk.
	Keep people focused and don't let them get sidetracked onto non-agenda items.
	Encourage contributions from all participants and don't let a small number of people dominate.
	Summarise views and decisions at the end of each item.
	Establish what will happen next and who will take action.
	Avoid too many items being raised as Any Other Business. Determine what can be moved forward to the next meeting's agenda.
	End the meeting on a positive note, thank participants and set the time and location of the next meeting, if appropriate.
After the meeting	Make sure that minutes are written up and circulated promptly.
	Monitor agreed action points to make sure that they are progressed.

Table 2.1 *The responsibilities and tasks of a meeting leader*

Source: adapted from Barker (1997), Guirdham (1995) and Hindle (1998)

An effective leader must have good communication skills across a variety of media; they should be able to listen, read non-verbal signals as well as speak fluently. They also need a range of interpersonal skills to help them to facilitate the group working together, drawing people in and controlling others.

◆ Assertiveness and the ability to control others without being aggressive.

◆ Fair-mindedness to ensure that all views are given equal consideration.

◆ Flexibility in dealing with different types of people.

◆ Openness and a willingness to listen to opinions you don't agree with.

◆ Organisational skills to ensure that everything is in place before the meeting and is fulfilled afterwards.

◆ Time management skills to ensure that the meeting runs to plan.

♦ The ability to delegate and enthuse others with a desire to complete tasks.

There are a number of ways a meeting leader can abuse their position and disrupt the outcomes of the meeting.

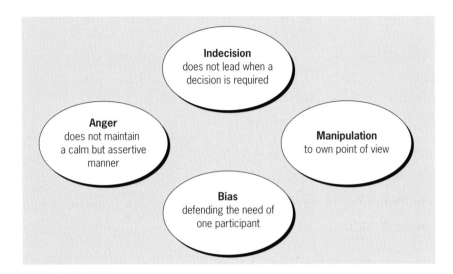

Figure 2.3 *Four ways a leader might abuse their position (adapted from Hindle, 1998)*

Problematic participants

One of the ways in which you can make your meetings more effective is to recognise the types of personality some problem participants might adopt as part of their meeting camouflage. You may be able to pin-point people from your experience that fall into these six groups identified by Hodgson and Hodgson (1993):

1. **Whisperers** mutter to colleagues and thus distract attention away from the speaker. You may be able to control them with non-verbal signals – looking at them or gesticulating – or you may have to speak directly to them. Suggest that they listen to the speaker and then you will ask them to speak. Avoid being challenging or sarcastic since this may stimulate a 'rebellious child' response and make the culprit even more of a distraction.

2. **Whingers** always find fault and appear to take pleasure in revealing drawbacks to proposals. Thank them for their contribution – and ask them how they think the problem can be resolved. This combination of recognition and flattery may encourage them to take a more constructive approach.

3. **Why Me's?** may be vocal during discussion but loath to participate in any action. Acknowledge how busy they are, then use open questions to determine what contributions they think they should make.

4. **Wanderers** stray from the subject under discussion and often lapse into reminiscences about their own experience. They need to be firmly controlled – stop them politely as soon as they begin and move on.

5. **Wizards** know everything and believe that they can speak with authority on any subject. Don't be fooled into thinking that they can achieve all they believe they can. Delegate responsibility for future action fairly among all participants.

6. **Worriers** look for problems. Use their doom-mongering positively by asking them to carry out risk analyses related to specific tasks.

However carefully you prepare for a meeting, you may still face problems that arise because of conflicts of interest or clashes of personality. Although you may find these difficult to deal with, these strategies may help.

◆ Repeat the objective of the meeting/item and ask people to focus on that.

◆ Avoid getting into arguments.

◆ Don't interrupt people.

◆ Set the tone, pitch and speed of the proceedings and don't mirror other people's behaviour. If they are getting heated and their voices are rising, it is essential that you slow proceeding down and stay calm.

◆ Focus on solutions rather than problems.

◆ Turn complaints into objectives by asking people to restate them as 'how to' statements.

◆ Praise useful contributions.

◆ If you need to criticise, criticise the remark not the speaker.

◆ Ask for different points of view.

◆ Don't allow participants to discuss people who are not at the meeting.

Derived from Barker (1997)

Following up the meeting

Once a meeting is over, the leader or organiser still has work to do.

◆ Make sure the minutes or notes are written up and circulated. These should include the date, time and venue for the next meeting if there is to be one.

◆ Monitor action. During the meeting, participants may have agreed to take on certain responsibilities and these should be noted in the minutes. Agreeing to do something isn't the same as actually doing it. Before the next meeting you should monitor their progress and be alert for any problems that could prevent them achieving their objectives.

An effective leader will also want to get feedback on his or her performance. This can be difficult; asking all participants to fill in a questionnaire assessing your leadership skills won't enhance your authority. The best strategy is to discuss the meeting informally with a participant that you trust to give you a fair evaluation. Avoid being drawn into discussions about individuals, but focus on assessing:

◆ the effectiveness of your introductory address

◆ time keeping

◆ whether objectives were achieved

◆ whether everybody had a fair chance to contribute

◆ outcomes – will agreed actions be carried out?

Video, teleconferencing, IM and online forums

Digital technology means that meetings with a number of people at remote locations are becoming increasingly normal. Some meetings take place asynchronously (virtual), ie over a defined period of time, but not necessarily with everyone present at one time. Virtual meetings have obvious benefits: they save time since participants don't have to travel to and from a specific venue, and therefore save money. The drawbacks relate to the level of competence of the people involved. For instance, if you have never participated in a video conference, it can be difficult to adjust your speaking and listening style to cope with the technology.

Video conferencing

During a video conference, you are on camera. Because of the remote transmission, there may be a gap between speaking and receiving similar to the delay on long distance telephone calls. To compensate for this, you need to speak more slowly and deliberately than usual. You also need to be patient: quickfire retorts and responses won't work on a system that takes a few seconds for your words to go down the line.

Video conferencing tips

◆ If you are organising a web conference, make sure that your IT team is briefed. They should take care of the equipment, carry out sound checks and be available in case anything goes wrong.

◆ Circulate documentation in advance, and include details of any presentations and copies of PowerPoint images.

- Start the conference with a sound and camera check for all participants.

- Always start your contribution by saying your name so people know who is speaking.

- Talk at a normal pitch and tone. The microphone means that you don't need to raise your voice.

- Watch your audience in the same way that you would if they were in the room. Check for signs of boredom or distraction and try to get them involved by asking questions or inviting comments.

- Allow for the slight delay in transmission when you are waiting for a response. Let someone finish what they are saying before you speak.

- Do not interrupt as this will cut them off mid-sentence. Remember that two people cannot speak at the same time.

- Stay in one place so that the camera is trained on you throughout the conference.

- Use the mute button if you need to discuss something off camera.

- Finally, avoid wearing strongly patterned clothes as these will distort and break-up on screen.

Tele/audio conferencing

This is the live exchange of information among participants using audio equipment. It is relatively cheap, simple and widely used. The guidelines for effective use of audio conferencing are similar to those for video conferencing except that you will not have the benefit of the visual cues from people's faces.

The main drawback of this form of communication is that when people are working in multiple locations and you have groups in each location it is easy to think that silences are more significant than they may actually be. A good leader is essential on these calls to orchestrate contributions. Never underestimate the power of using names to gain attention and invite contributions. Your own name is difficult to ignore.

With the synchronised use of computer equipment it is also relatively easy to use data sharing to display and send information and graphics to accompany the call.

Data conferencing

Data conferencing is a powerful means of sharing information. The sharing process demands high levels of preparation, but provides high returns for participants. Wikipedia describes data conferencing as follows.

> Data Conferencing refers to a communication session among two or more participants sharing computer data in real time. Interaction and presentation devices such as a screen, keyboard, mouse, camera, etc. can be shared or be able to control each other's computer. It is used to distinguish it from video conferencing and audio conferencing.
>
> The data can include screen, documents, graphics, drawings and applications that can be seen, annotated or manipulated by participants.

Source: http://en.wikipedia.org/wiki/Data_conferencing
(accessed October 2006)

Instant messaging

Instant messaging or IM is a form of real-time communication. It can occur between two or more people and is based on text typed and sent instantly. The text is sent via computers connected over a network such as the Internet. The possibilities for IM are growing and popular, because with an existing network in place the messages are free of charge. Real-time text discussions harness people's ability to multi-task and break through typical communication barriers to increase productivity. For example, a user can be on the phone with a customer while using IM to gather necessary information from others in the organisation to help solve a problem or close a sale.

Instant messages can be sent via mobile phones as well as land lines. Most services tell you whether participants are present and include contact lists and groups. The main disadvantages are that with multiple users the messages can appear out of sequence leading to multiple conversation threads, but for most this adds to the interest, and that people can be tracked via their IM presence status.

As use of the medium grows and latest approximate estimates are in the region of 13 billion messages per day (2005) with over 500 million users potential risks are beginning to emerge, especially for corportate users. Microsoft have identified some potential risks associated with IM in the workplace as follows:

- The organisation has little or no control over how IM applications are used and implemented. Public IM applications cannot be easily 'locked' to constrain the types of messages sent or with whom they may be exchanged.

- The lack of interoperability between major IM applications makes standardisation difficult. Users may have to install multiple IM clients to communicate with all of their intended parties.

- As both legitimate and unapproved use of instant messaging clients and peer-to-peer networking increases, new worms and viruses are increasingly using these mechanisms to spread.

- IM interactions are not easily captured, logged, or audited. After the client software is closed, messages are typically deleted. Hence, these messages do not become part of any interaction history, and thus the information cannot be mined or used for customer relationship management (CRM) or compliance purposes.

Management and Security Considerations for Instant Messaging in the Workplace Microsoft Corporation Published: December 2005

The possibilities of the media and its popularity, however, look set to see instant messaging thrive and grow in organisations.

Online forums

Online forums are a useful source of information to millions of people. They are probably less commonly used by organisations, because of a perceived need to keep information secure. Intranets may include online forums, but a requirement to ensure that false or defamatory comments are avoided means that constant monitoring is required.

If you are using a forum the following principles may be of assistance.

- Respect the audience. That includes not spamming, flaming, selling e-mail information etc.

- Simple communication is better. If you can say it simply why make it complicated? No one on the web has time to research every other word or read humongous documents. Bulleted lists and simple graphics are easy to scan.

- Think in community, but cater to the individual.

- Words can easily be misinterpreted and come across the wrong way.

- Don't do anything online that you wouldn't do offline.

Activity 6
Evaluate your skills as a meeting leader

Objective

This activity encourages you to evaluate your skills as a leader. You may want to try this activity using a tele/audio or video conference or an asynchronous web chat to see how the styles vary.

Task

1. *The first part of this activity should be completed before the meeting.* Look at the agenda and briefly evaluate what the meeting as a whole should achieve. Then consider the objectives for individual agenda items. Use action words to denote what you want to do: 'agree...', 'finalise...', 'complete...', etc.

2. Check the technology if you are using it and look up some guidelines on the internet if it's new to you.

3. Identify possible areas of agreement and dispute. By doing this in advance, you will be better equipped to handle controversial issues during the meeting.

4. Look at a list of the people taking part and consider the contributions that they could make during the meeting. Who is likely to dominate? Who may be reticent and need drawing out? What strategies will you use to ensure that everyone has a fair chance to participate?

5. Using Hodgson and Hodgson's (1993) definitions, identify the various types of meeting participant. What is likely to be their individual areas of concern?

6. Your final task is to prepare an opening for the meeting. Make notes of the points you want to highlight – both in terms of the content of the meeting and the behaviour you expect from the participants.

7. *The second part of the activity should be completed after the meeting.* Complete the self-assessment test to evaluate your performance as a leader.

1 Objectives for the meeting as a whole and individual agenda items

2   Possible areas of agreement

Possible areas of dispute

3   Which participants are likely to dominate? How will you deal with them?

Which participants are likely to take a back seat? How will you deal with them?

4 Type	Person/area of concern
Whisperer	
Whinger	
Why Me?	
Wanderer	
Wizard	
Worrier	

5   Opening address

6   Consider each of the statements in this chart and rate your performance.

	Very poor	Poor	OK	Good	Very good
Practical preparation before the meeting (agenda, venue etc.)	☐	☐	☐	☐	☐
Familiarisation with agenda items, minutes and papers	☐	☐	☐	☐	☐
Familiarisation with meeting participants (their characters, interests, views, likely conflicts)	☐	☐	☐	☐	☐
Opening the meeting (start on time, welcome, introductions, state aims, positive start)	☐	☐	☐	☐	☐
Pacing the meeting (keeping to timings)	☐	☐	☐	☐	☐
Thinking on your feet, for example, in deciding whether to overrun the time for an item in the light of new information	☐	☐	☐	☐	☐
Facilitating items (introducing, listening, encouraging contributions, summarising, agreeing action)	☐	☐	☐	☐	☐
Dealing with difficult situations (dominant person, conflict, etc.)	☐	☐	☐	☐	☐
Dealing with AOB (keep to minimum)	☐	☐	☐	☐	☐
Closing the meeting (end positively, summarise decisions and actions, thanks, date of next meeting)	☐	☐	☐	☐	☐
Following up afterwards (writing and circulating minutes, monitoring progress on action)	☐	☐	☐	☐	☐

Feedback

If you are meeting people you know reasonably well, you should have been able to identify potential problems before the meeting. Knowledge is power: knowing what you will have to deal with in advance will help you to develop coping strategies.

Check your opening and make sure it:

◆ refers to relevant past events/background information

◆ clearly states why the meetings has been convened

◆ determine specific objectives and outcomes

◆ clarifies the amount of time you have

◆ states any controls that you want to impose (e.g. making contributions via the leader, taking questions at the end of presentations, etc.).

As well as reviewing your performance as leader, you could also ask a colleague who participated in the meeting to use the test to give you their feedback. Focus on areas where you rated less than 'good': how can you develop your skills to improve your rating?

◆ Recap

Consider the value and limitations of meetings as a means of exchanging information and making decisions

◆ Meetings are effective in imparting information, eliciting views and stimulating new ideas, and for team motivation and reaching decisions. They aren't always the best way to communicate with colleagues, however. Always consider whether a meeting is absolutely necessary before you convene one.

Prepare to participate in meetings and use your speaking and listening skills to contribute effectively

A meeting may fail because of inadequate planning and preparation, low levels of participation by the members or poor leadership. The meeting may also fail if the participants feel that it is unnecessary.

◆ If you are organising a meeting, clarify: what the meeting is about; who will attend; when and where it will take place. Be guided by the needs of the participants and always maintain a focus on what the desired outcome of the meeting will be.

- Whether you are participating or leading a meeting, you will need to prepare by studying the previous minutes and agenda, and assessing how your contribution will move the proceedings forward.

- To participate effectively, you need to keep an open mind, respect and listen actively to the contribution of others, be willing to challenge when you are not convinced and take notes.

Prepare to lead a meeting and follow up relevant action points afterwards

- Leading a meeting involves ensuring that it achieves its objectives and getting the best out of the participants.

- Effective leading is achieved by: adopting an authoritative approach; giving succinct summaries; using the skills of listening, questioning and reading body language to encourage contribution from all participants; and being open and fair-minded to ensure all views are aired and given equal consideration.

▶▶ More @

You'll find more practical techniques on how to achieve results through meetings in any of the following texts:

Barker, A. (1997) *How to Hold Better Meetings*, **Kogan Page**

Hindle, T. (1998) *Managing Meetings*, **Dorling Kindersley**

Hodgson, P. and Hodgson, J. (1992) *Effective Meetings*, **Century Business**

Lencioni, P. (2004), *Death by Meeting*, **Pfeiffer Wiley**
In this leadership fable, the protagonists are the boss, Casey, and an employee named Will who eventually loses his temper in the face of one more stifling, useless meeting.

Full references are provided at the end of the book.

3 Written communications

We process large amounts of written text every day. The newspapers we read, the messages on advertising hoardings, texts, emails, instant messages, junk mail and reports – these are just a fraction of the written communications that we deal with. Small wonder then, that we often skim-read and don't give important material the attention it deserves or consider our own messages adequately.

> So fast, spontaneous and informal is the medium that many fire emails off without a second thought. The restraining influences of stamp-buying, envelope-licking and letter-delivering are gone. Now you just flick one off the wrist and see what happens.

Gary Younge, Guardian Unlimited
www.guardian.co.uk/Columnists/Column/0,,417599,00.html 2001

If communications are treated so lightly they are unlikely to gain the attention you may require. Any impersonal communication that you prepare will have to fight for your audience's attention; it is therefore essential that you write and present your material persuasively so that it achieves your objectives. In this section you will:

◆ consider the relevance of written communications and the most appropriate format to use in specific situations

◆ produce effective written communications to supply information or generate action

◆ use standard conventions and presentation, including business language, statistical/visual materials, and appendices when writing letters, memos, reports and emails.

Types of written communication

> The written word (including writing reports and letters, reading and taking notes), meetings, public presentations, exhibitions and conferences, email and other forms of electronic communication, information obtained/passed through the Internet or Intranet (internal, external – locally, nationally, internationally), facsimile, etc. are all examples of the impersonal communication with which managers must deal with effectively and efficiently.

Source: Murdock and Scutt (2003)

This table outlines the pros and cons of the main types of business documents that you will encounter.

Type of document	Good for	Not so good for
Letter	Providing a formal record	Getting a quick reply
Email or Blackberry/ PDA messages	Short messages Speed and getting a quick response Dispersing the same message to a large number of people Sending attachments – documents and graphics – capable of sending large files	Conveying several messages at the same time Confidential messages
Instant message	Quick knowledge and information sharing among a group or with an individual Non intrusive since you don't need to reply Getting a quick response Informal and often fun	Storing messages, logging ideas and thoughts Formal communications Long messages
Text/SMS	Mobile messaging – any time, any where Short messages Graphics and video attachments	Long messages
Fax	Documents that can't be sent electronically Signed documents Instant delivery	Communicating small/coloured print or detailed graphics
Report	Summarising information and views Presenting the facts, information and data Persuading people	Informal communication
Proposal	Presenting a case with supporting arguments	Communicating when it would be better to discuss issues first
Intranet message boards	Internal and non urgent messages Messages of interest to a specific group of people but of possible interest to others Social arrangements to a wide audience	Urgent messages Confidential messages
Graphics and pictures	Communicating an idea in a document or PowerPoint presentation Making complex information digestible	Documents that need to be prepared quickly – they can take a long time to format
Notice boards	Communicating with people on site	Dispersed team

Communication might be thought of as an 'idea transplant.' We send 300 to 1,000 messages a day. We probably receive that many messages too.

Marilyn Lesmeister
Leadership and Volunteer Development Specialist, NDSU Extension Service

Table 3.1 *Pros and cons of business communication methods*

The type of written communication you use will depend on your objectives and the culture in your organisation. For example, some workplaces rely heavily on electronic communication, others prefer more traditional letter writing. Here are some suggestions for appropriate methods.

Situation	Communication method
To warn a member of your team about shortfalls in performance	Letter – this is a warning and will need to be kept on record. You need to know that your team member has received it
To remind your team about the staff charity half-marathon at the end of the month	Email, text message, intranet
To remind all your team members that appraisal interviews start next week	Email, memo, staff notice board, intranet
To provide a supplier with a purchase order	Letter or fax will give them a written record. You could also email, if you know that the supplier is accustomed to receiving orders, etc. in this medium
To present the month's sales figures to senior management	Email, Report
To suggest a new format for product packaging	Presentation
To brainstorm some ideas for a new service with your team	Instant messaging, Blackberry/PDA messaging

Table 3.2 *Communication methods to match the purpose*

The format and structure of your document is influenced by its purpose and the needs of your audience.

Purpose

Before you write a document, you should be clear about:

- who you want to read it and what they already know
- what you want readers to do when they've read it
- what outcomes you want to achieve.

Written communication may be used to:

- change behaviour or beliefs
- answer a question
- present facts
- presents results
- describe situations
- provide information
- record past events
- recommend
- influence decision-making
- bring about action
- persuade.

Source: W.G. Hardy quoted in Murdock and Scutt (2003)

Audience

As with any form of communication, your audience's needs should influence the structure that you use. Stevens (1989) suggests that before you start to write, you find out your audience's:

- level of education
- first language – English or not?
- profession
- level of authority
- knowledge of the subject
- interest in the subject
- professional and personal needs
- organisation's culture (conservative, informal, etc.).

You should also consider your audience's attitudes and the ways in which they are likely to receive what you are saying. All these factors will help to determine the format to which your audience will be most responsive. It is pointless relying on text or email to communicate with a technophobe, or writing in language specific to your profession to a group of laypersons.

Write it so they'll read it

Taylor (2000) advises using the five Ws to determine the focus of your writing and plan a communication.

Who?

Who is my reader?

What is my relationship with my reader?

When?

When does my reader need the information?

When should I start this document?

When is the deadline?

When do I need a reply?

What?

What message do I want to convey?

What does my reader know already?

What does my reader need to know?

What does my reader expect of me?

How can I help my reader understand?

What are my reader's attitudes and how can I turn these to my advantage?

Where?
Where can I find the information that my reader needs?
Where is the reader (this will influence your choice of communication method)

Why?
Why is the subject important to me?
How does it contribute to my goals?
Why should the reader pay attention to me?
Why should the reader *not* pay attention to me?
Why does my reader need this information?
Why might my reader be interested in this topic?
Why might my reader *not* be interested in this topic?

Table 3.3 *The five Ws for writing*   Adapted from Taylor (2000: page 81)

Activity 7
Plan a written communication

Use the questions associated with the five Ws to focus on a written communication that you intend to produce.

Who?

When?

What?

Where?

Why?

Using your answers, define:

The format for your communication (letter, fax, report, email, etc.)

Its key messages

Its approximate length

Factors that will influence your style/language

Feedback

Clarifying the five Ws will help you to determine the best medium for your communication and establish certain guidelines that will help you to structure the content.

Structure and tone

Once you have considered the purpose of your document and chosen an appropriate medium, you can structure it. Strengthen your case, whether you are presenting it in a brief email or a lengthy report, by:

◆ prioritising information – put the most important information first where it will have the most impact

◆ carefully selecting what to include and omit – there is no room for waffle

◆ including your recommendations and indicating what should or will happen next.

A written document should be straightforward. As with any other communication form:

◆ tell them what you're going to tell them

◆ tell them

◆ tell them what you've told them.

This translates into:

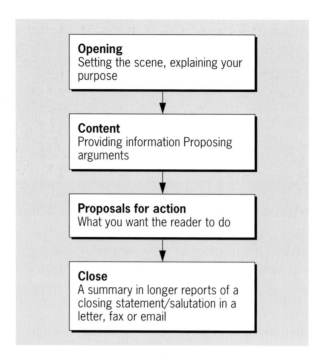

Figure 3.1 *Template for written communication*

Getting the right tone

Once you have outlined your structure, you can choose the appropriate language, style and tone to convey your message. In verbal communication, when you can observe non-verbal signals, words are often less important than the way in which they are spoken. In written communications, it is the words themselves that carry the impact so you must use them with care. Common errors include being:

♦ aggressive and making demands

♦ patronising and 'talking down' to the reader

♦ dismissive and not taking the reader's reactions into account

♦ critical when the reader cannot respond to what you say.

Always read a document before you send it and put yourself in the reader's shoes. How would you feel if this letter/report/email appeared on your desk?

Using business English

The increasing use of email and text messages has encouraged the use of less formal language and style in business communications. When writing letters, reports or proposals, however, you will generate more respect and attention if you use a more formal style that avoids colloquialisms and uses grammar accurately. This doesn't mean that the end result has to be turgid or complex.

By employing the Keeping It Short and Simple (KISS) principle you can communicate formally but still produce a highly readable document.

◆ Use straightforward language and avoid jargon and complex words that your audience may not be familiar with.

◆ Use active rather than passive language. 'We believe...' has more impact than 'It is a generally accepted fact within the company...'

◆ Avoid complicated or lengthy sentences. Murdock and Scutt (2003) suggest that you aim for 10-20 words per sentence, and three to five sentences per paragraph.

◆ Use separate sentences to express different ideas. Don't lose the thread of an argument by interrupting it with statements in brackets, commas and dashes.

◆ State ideas and concepts directly – don't embellish unless necessary.

> **The chief virtue that language can have is clearness and nothing detracts from it so much as unfamiliar words**
> **Hippocrates**

Needlessly complicated:
Technical assistance to institutional administrative staff is authorised in determination of the ability and appropriate untilisation of federal or state entitlements designating assistance in resolution of problems occassioned by requirements of handicapped children. [33 words]

In plain English:
We can help your staff determine if federal or state funds are available to help meet the needs of handicapped children. We can help you plan how best to use those funds. [32 words]

Oversimplified:
We can help you get government money and we can help you spend it. [14 words]

Source: Joseph (1998)

Presentation

The way you present your information will depend on to whom you are sending it and the importance of the communication. There are standard formats for letters, reports and even emails – even if only a subject heading, a greeting and a sign off. You may have a house style and templates that will help you to set them out properly. In a lengthy document, use bullet points or sub-headings to break up the text and focus your audience on key points.

Title:
clear, bold type

Type:
left aligned type is easy to
read, consistent use of font

Sub-headings:
to break up the text and
provide direction

Numbers and bullets:
use to help legibility

Blue Sky Marketing Plan
Blue Sky's Best Opportunity for East Region Expansion

Summary

In focusing on the opportunities for Eastern Region expansion, this report considers both the potential to replicate the Southern business model and the prospect for taking space in Omega's stores. Partnering Omega is the recommended option for two reasons:

● They already have an excellent infrastructure of stores that would enable us to achieve an estimated 70% penetration by March 2007.

● The Eastern Region will be profitable by the end of 2008 as oppose to 2010 if we develop our own infrastructure.

Introduction

In December 2005, the Exley consultancy were commissioned to explore opportunities for expansion into the Eastern Region with the following objectives were set for the project:

● Identify predicted demand for products in code bands Z/14333 to K/1029

● Assess most effective way to develop store infrastructure that would enable Blue Sky to achieve £5m in revenue and move into profit by 2008

● Evaluate potential risks associated with East region expansion.

This report considers their findings in five main sections:

● The Eastern Region – demographics and socio-economic profile of customers and staff

● Analysis of competitive environment

● Expanding into the Eastern Region – revenue and profit model

● Partnering Omega – revenue and profit model

● Recommendations and proposed plan of action.

06/01/2007   1

Figure 3.2 *Presentation and layout*

Graphics and a layout with short line lengths will make any document more easy to read. If you are using email or IM consider whether emoticons, icons or graphics could help you get your particular message across better or appropriately.

Editing

The key here is that less is more. Think about whether you can leave some messages unsaid to help engage your audience, whether a few questions might raise issues you hadn't thought of. The first task of editing is to ensure that the key points are not being lost amidst the plethora of points you are trying to make.

Few of us have the skill to write perfectly without some revision and editing. You should always check your document against you original plan to ensure that it fits its purpose. Then check for:

- Grammatical mistakes
- Typographical and spelling mistakes
- Unnecessary punctuation: read sentences out loud to check that commas, semi-colons, etc, are used for a purpose.

A panda walks into a cafe. He orders a sandwich, eats it, then draws a gun and fires two shots in the air.

'Why?' asks the confused waiter, as the panda makes towards the exit. The panda produces a badly punctuated wildlife manual and tosses it over his shoulder.

'I'm a panda,' he says at the door. 'Look it up.'

The waiter turns to the relevant entry and, sure enough, finds an explanation.

'**Panda.** Large black-and-white bear-like mammal native to China. Eats, shoots and leaves.'

Source: Truss (2005)

Accurate grammar and spelling really do matter; they reflect on your thoroughness and reliability. If you can't be bothered to write an accurate letter or email, why should a client trust you to get their order right?

Word-processing spell and grammar checks have made life much easier. Beware of relying on them too heavily, however – their accuracy is dependant on the skills of the person using them. The following slips represent the commonest kind of mistakes that are not caught by a spell check:

- I have a spelling chequer
- It cam with my PC
- It planely marks four my revue
- Miss Takes eye cannot sea
- I've run this poem threw it
- I'm shore your please to no
- Its letter perfect in every weigh
- My chequer tolled me sew

Source: Unknown, quoted in Taylor (2000)

Edit ruthlessly: don't include phrases simply because you like the sound of them. If they don't make an active contribution to your message, take them out.

Writing reports

A report, proposal or other lengthy document should be set out with as much care and attention as any other document – and this takes time. Make sure that you start your preparation as early as possible; these documents invariably take longer to compile than you expect and if you complete them in a hurry, you are unlikely to end up with a finished product that you can be proud of.

Whatever the length of the document, it should be easy for the reader to scan quickly and get the gist of. It may be useful to include an executive summary or abstract at the start of the report that summarises its objectives and conclusions. You can also transfer detailed research and supporting information into appendices, so that the body of the report remains reasonably concise.

Your organisation may have a house style that dictates the content of reports. Otherwise, you could use this sample format.

1 Title page

2 Table of contents

3 Executive summary

4 Your key messages and your findings

5 Conclusion and recommendations

6 Appendices.

Break down the content by using headings, sub-headings and bullets. These provide a 'break' for your reader so that they can cut off and move to another point, and will help you to highlight key points. You can also foster your audience's attention by using graphic communications and statistical presentation methods.

Murdock and Scutt (2003) define graphic communication as: 'the use of visual techniques to aid communication' and define four distinct types:

1 Lettering and typography

2 Illustration and design

3 Graphic enhancement – signs and icons

4 Maps and diagrams.

Figure 3.3 *The impact of graphics*

'We now live in a rich visual culture, and, in a technological and fast-changing world, we are used to dealing with huge amounts of information. We learnt long ago that much information can be assimilated quickly, and that graphic design and logos can help to carry numerous and simple messages with essential impact.'

Murdock and Scutt (2003)

Avoid the temptation to over-complicate your document, however; too many different fonts and icons can be irritating rather than effective.

Statistical presentation of numerical data can give a snapshot of a situation to a reader and thus will have more impact than columns of figures. Software packages will help you to create pie, bar and line charts.

Taylor (2000) suggests the following tips for creating effective business reports.

◆ They should be useful, factual, objective, well-organised and well-presented.

◆ Classify findings under headings and sub-headings and be consistent in presentation and spacing.

◆ Use numbered points.

◆ Make sure that all sentences follow the same grammatical pattern (e.g. don't switch from third to first person).

◆ Be concise, stick to the point and avoid long explanations.

◆ Check that information is accurate and reasoning valid.

◆ Use a simple presentation that will help the reader to understand the content.

◆ In less formal or memo reports, use a more relaxed style if appropriate.

Source: Adapted from Taylor (2000)

Activity 8
Evaluate a report

Select a report that you have written or received recently and evaluate it using the criteria in this table. In the fourth column suggest any improvements that would make the report easier to read.

	Yes	No	Suggested improvements
Uses a logical format	☐	☐	
Summarises key points clearly in an executive summary or introduction	☐	☐	
Make it clear who wrote the report and when?	☐	☐	
Uses appropriate graphic and statistical presentation methods to facilitate understanding	☐	☐	
Breaks up the text with headings, bullet points, etc.	☐	☐	
Uses accessible language and minimal jargon	☐	☐	
Clearly explains acronyms and technical terms	☐	☐	
Uses appropriate punctuation, sentence structure and spelling	☐	☐	
Includes appropriate appendices	☐	☐	

Feedback

Hopefully this activity will have focused you attention on the details of writing a report. Many reports fall short of the desired standard. They are confused, badly presented and carry too much detail that detracts from the central messages. To prepare a well-written and presented report takes time – it will probably go through a number of draft versions before it is ready for circulation. If you found that the report you analysed was below par it may well have been rushed.

◆ Recap

Consider the relevance of written communications and choose the most appropriate format to use in specific situations

- ◆ The format you choose for a written communication should reflect its purpose and suit its audience.

Produce effective written communications to supply information or generate action

- ◆ All written communications – however short or informal – require planning and preparation. Determine who the communication is for, when it will be received, where you will find the necessary information to include in it, what it is intended to do and why you are writing it.

- ◆ Documents should be structured logically and include an opening, content, an indication of the required response and a summary.

Use standard conventions and presentation, including business language, statistical/visual materials, and appendices when writing letters, memos, reports and emails

- ◆ The language you use will depend on the culture in your organisation and that of the recipient. Some organisations use a more formal style than others.

- ◆ The KISS rule applies, even to lengthy or complex documents. Keep it as short and simple as possible.

- ◆ Writing a report takes time and thorough preparation. Reports that fail to convey their message have often been prepared in a hurry.

- ◆ They should follow a logical format and clearly state their intent in their introduction and summary.

- Use appendices to include detailed information that needs to be incorporated in the report but could detract from the central arguments.

- Presentation is important in a long document. Break up the content by using headings and sub-headings, bullet points, graphics and statistical presentation methods.

▶▶ More @

www.businessballs.com has a section offering general tips for all types of writing including letters, sales literature and reports.

www.mindtools.com also includes valuable information on writing and proofing documents.

A range of excellent books on written communication are available including:

Leigh, A. and Maynard, M. (1993) *Perfect Communications*, Arrow Books

Joseph, A. (1998) *Put it in Writing, Learn how to Write Clearly, Quickly and Persuasively*, Mcgraw Hill
Provides tips and features interactive exercises that strengthen skills in organising letters and reports; supercharging language; avoiding lazy grammar; using computers to improve skills.

Truss, L. (2003) *Eats Shoots & Leaves*, Profile Books
A readable and amusing book on the value of punctuation

Taylor, S. (2000) *Essential Communication Skills*, Longman
An excellent book on both written and oral communcation

4 | **Making presentations**

The purpose of presentations is to send and receive information, but to do it in a way that makes people WANT to hear what you say. Getting your message across is more than just saying the right things.

As a manager it is likely that you have to make presentations. The power and opportunity we are given each time we present before an audience or even sit around a table with a captive group of people is huge. But for many of us presenting is an intimidating experience that leads us to forget about our audience and to focus instead on ourselves. As with other forms of communication, thorough preparation can make the job easier. You might also want to consider the advice of management writer Philip Crosby.

No one can remember more than three points.

In this section you will find out how to plan and deliver a presentation to your colleagues. You will:

◆ prepare to deliver a presentation by defining your objectives, analysing the audience and any constraints that might impact on your performance

◆ plan a presentation (including logistics, style, structure, content and media)

◆ consider factors that will help you to deliver the presentation effectively, adapting to circumstances as relevant and responding appropriately to questions

◆ review own performance, and develop own presentation skills accordingly.

Planning a presentation

As technology becomes more sophisticated – and more interesting to use – the method of delivering presentations sometimes detracts from their meaning. The focus becomes the challenge of using computer hardware and software rather than clearly conveying the message.

A presentation is a means by which you present a problem or report in a structured way in a face-to-face setting. It is also an exercise in persuasion, since you want your audience to accept the message that you are delivering. You may, for example, want them to agree a course of action or modify their attitudes.

Presentations can be an effective way to communicate information to a group of people; they can also be boring, overly complex (probably more than three points), and fail to hold the attention of the audience. If you want to pass on a large amount of complex information, it may be more productive to circulate a report that audience members can digest in their own time. You may also have attended presentations that told you nothing you didn't know already, where a simple memo or phone call would have served to gauge your response.

What people really want from a presentation, and this distinguishes it from a report, is the person attached to it. They want to hear what you have to say with all your body language, your voice and your idiosyncrasies.

Presentations should not be used:

♦ to fill in time at meetings

♦ as a substitute for discussion about sensitive or contentious issues

♦ to avoid one-to-one dialogues that may be difficult or uncomfortable.

They are your opportunity to tell people what you think, what you want them to think, in other words to persuade them of your views. Franklin D Roosevelt said, 'Be sincere, be brief, be seated.' Reflect this in your presentation and you are likely to find it works.

Planning a presentation requires some more thought.

Use the five Ws to determine:

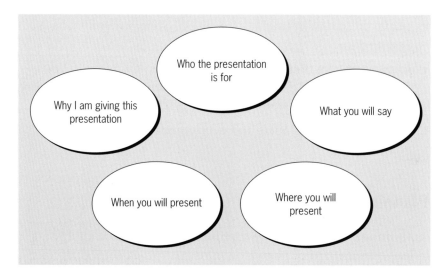

Figure 4.1 *The five Ws of presenting*

Why?

Murdock and Scutt (2003: page 64) suggest that it is necessary to ask:

♦ What the purpose of the presentation is for you?

♦ What is its purpose for your audience?

There may be differences between the two. You need to consider your audience's expectations since this will influence your content and delivery. If your intention is to influence your audience, then you must meet their needs rather than focusing on your own.

You need to clearly define your objective before you can plan the content of our presentation and set this out in one sentence. For example, it may be 'to persuade staff to accept a change in our management structure' or 'to showcase a new product to clients and persuade them to try it'. By defining your objective, you'll clarify your thoughts and provide a focus against which you can check your content as the presentation develops – it will help you stick to the point. One of the biggest problems in presentations is that speakers try to achieve too much and their central message is diluted.

> **Objectives are a security blanket to protect you from rambling.**
> **Wess Roberts**
> **Author of Leadership Secrets of Attila the Hun.**

Who?

Your audience will influence the way you speak; for example, we tend to address colleagues differently to clients because we assume that the former share our cultural influences and objectives. The size of the audience is also a factor. Establishing rapport with any size of audience needs to be planned; can you address them less formally, how can you gauge their reaction and how will you deal effectively with questions and feedback?

The knowledge levels and mood of your audience will also influence your delivery style. If they have little background knowledge about the subject, you may have to go back to basics and simplify your presentation. If the audience is likely to be confrontational, you will need to structure arguments carefully and anticipate their areas of concern.

What?

You will know a lot more about your subject than you need for your presentation. Walters (1993) indicates that a week after your presentation, your audience will remember only 20% of what they have heard. So you need keep your presentations short and simple (KISS). Sort through all the ideas and material you would love to talk about and boil it down to a basic message with **3 main points, if possible,** that are most vital to getting your message across.

> **Be audience driven, organize each point starting with the audience's needs.**
> **Somers White**
> **Author, Speaker, Arizona State Senator**

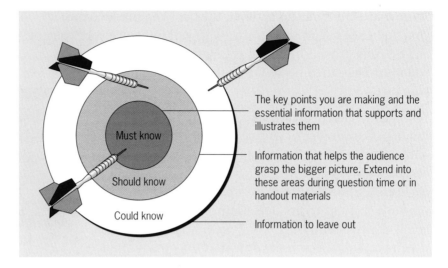

Figure 5.2 *Hit the target*

When?

The timing of a presentation will be linked to a number of factors:

◆ Audience availability; there's no point in giving a presentation at a time of day when the people you want to interact with can't be present.

◆ Factors relating to the content: for example, if you are introducing a new product at what point in its launch will you present it to potential customers? If you showcase it too soon you won't be able to fulfil orders; if you wait too long, you may produce too much of the product before you know whether customers will buy it.

Where?

The venue for your presentation should be appropriate for the size of the audience. Consider the options for running the presentation online or via video conferencing. It's your space and you need to plan how you are going to use it. If it is a physical venue you need to be sure its spacious enough for everyone to sit comfortably and for them to see visual aids if you are using them. On the other hand, presenting to a small audience with whom you want to develop a rapport could be difficult if the venue is too large or formal.

Using visual aids, pictures and props

 Technology can make a presentation easier to understand and create a strong impact – if it works and you know how to use it properly. Watching a presenter fiddle with his computer, try to get the lighting right so that the audience can see the screen, or use badly written slides, is distracting and annoying for the audience and can erode their confidence in what the speaker has to say.

Your choice of visual aids should be dictated by the following.

◆ What you want to say: don't use unnecessary illustrations. For instance illustrate the most important point with an action or prop, and the second key point with a picture.

◆ Your audience: would they find it more useful to read the information you want to impart? Can they get involved in helping you to get your messages across. For instance putting fact cards in envelopes and distributing them to people as they come in creates a sense of anticipation and participation.

◆ The space in which you are presenting. Can everyone see the screen? Can the room be blacked out sufficiently? Can they all see you and see each other?

Visual presentation methods should never be used as a substitute for good content or an appropriate speaking style. Experts are divided about their usefulness.

Arguments for using visual aids:	Arguments against using visual aids:
They can support an reinforce your spoken words.	They can distract the audience and stop them listening to you.
They can be used to summarise key points.	If they are simply repeating points that you are stating, why are you using them?
Copies can be given to the audience as handouts so that they have clear reminders of the presentation after the event. They may distract the audience form what you are saying.	People listen at the same rate but read at different rates.
Props can be used to illustrate a point. For instance using physical steps to illustrate a process. Using posters in a gallery to build up a picture.	This can have a lot of impact if used sparingly, but make sure it doesn't patronise.

Table 4.1 *Using visual aids*

Visual aids that succeed are:

◆ short and snappy with no more than five or six points per slide

◆ big enough to read – use an appropriate font size

◆ adding value, break-up the presentation and make it more interesting

◆ used sparingly – no more than one slide per three minutes of formal presentation time

◆ not based on numerical tables – these will be too complex for your audience to absorb

◆ not crowded with graphics, fancy headings or complex fonts

◆ accurate and have correct spelling, grammar and punctuation – if they are badly presented your audience may lose confidence in what you are saying.

PowerPoint slides are just one of a range of presentation aids you could use. Consider:

◆ video

◆ writing or drawing on flipcharts

◆ models that you can hand round

◆ photographs

◆ handouts

◆ music to add mood and impact

◆ posters to reinforce key messages both before and after the presentation

◆ webpages

◆ intranet/internet links, etc.

If you are unfamiliar with the presentation methods that are available in your organisation, arrange for some training from an expert. It will prove a valuable investment since not only will it open up a new world of technology that you could find useful, but it will also build your confidence.

Activity 9
Plan and prepare a presentation

Objective

In this activity, you will plan and prepare a presentation that you will deliver at the end of this section.

Task

1. Using the boxes below, make brief notes to clarify the who, what, when and where of your presentation.

Who?

Make brief notes about your audience.

How many people will be there?

Who are they?

What is their level of understanding about the subject?

Will they be receptive or antipathetic to your presentation?

What?

Define the objective of your presentation in one sentence.

When?

When will you give the presentation? How does the timing relate to the content?

Where?

Where will you give the presentation? What are your reasons for choosing this space?

Visual aids

What visual and presentation aids will you use? Give a reason for each one. For example, if you are planning to use a flipchart, explain why.

2. You have now defined the objective of your presentation. The next stage is to break this down into a workable structure.

Write down the topic areas that you need to cover and bullet point the key points for each one.

Devise a logical order for presenting the different sections. Start with some scene setting (how much will depend on the knowledge of your audience), move on to specific issues and end by indicating what will happen next.

Allocate time for each section. If you are short of time, which sections can be cut?

Feedback

This activity used a simple evaluation procedure to clarify your thoughts about your presentation. Make sure that you have completed each section before you move on to preparing the detailed content, since the five Ws will influence what you actually say. You may not be able to include everything you hoped — remember that the success of the presentation depends to a large extent on how you relate to your audience. If you try to tell them too much you may lose their attention.

The audience attention curve

Timing is important. Jay and Jay (2000) state that psychologists have plotted the attention span of an audience over a 40-minute period. It starts high, drops quite shallowly for the first 10 minutes, then more steeply until it reached its lowest point after about 30 minutes. Towards the end, it starts to rise again, presumably as the audience realises that the end is in sight.

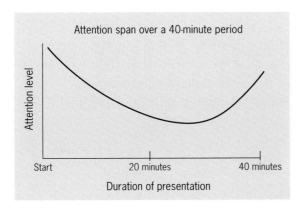

Figure 5.3 *The audience attention curve*   Source: Jay and Jay (2000)

The most effective presentation structure maps the audience attention curve and has a beginning, a middle and an end.

Beginning	Middle	End
Tell them what you're going to tell them	Tell them	Tell them what you told them
◆ Attention grabber	◆ Three key points	◆ Strong summary of purpose and key points
◆ The purpose of the talk	◆ Each point illustrated by evidence and examples	
◆ Presentation plan (preview of key points)		

Table 4.2 *The structure of a presentation*

Repetition helps. In Secrets of Successful Presenters, Walters (1993), quotes the following statistics regarding repeats and retention rate:

Number of repeats	Amount of retention
1	<10%
6	>90%

Table 4.3 *Repetition and retention rates*

Delivering a presentation

Some speakers can walk onto a podium, look at their audience and instantly gauge how that audience wants to be addressed. Most of us are not so skilled and need to plan how we will address the audience before we start.

Speaking style

Your speaking style will be influenced by the content of your presentation and by the audience. It may be formal and delivered to a large audience, in which case your language should be grammatically accurate and you may need a detailed script. It may be an informal presentation to a group of close colleagues, so you could probably use your normal speaking style and rely on some brief notes of key points. It may be something between the two. Whatever the style, maintain the general principles of good communication.

◆ Keep your language simple and direct.

◆ Use short sentences.

◆ Include a clear introduction and summary.

◆ Avoid jargon.

◆ Involve your audience by using rhetorical questions or asking for feedback.

◆ Use humour sparingly and only if you are confident that it will work with this particular audience.

◆ Control the pace of your delivery. If it's too slow your audience will get bored; if it's too fast, they won't understand you or be able to take notes.

Detailed preparation builds confidence; by the time you deliver your presentation you will know what you want to achieve and what you will say. Nevertheless, some of us will always find speaking to a group of people difficult. The following suggestions will help you to approach a presentation with equanimity.

Before you begin

◆ Wait until your audience is settled.

◆ Smile and make eye contact with them before you start speaking. Avoid focussing on the more influential or dominant members of your audience.

◆ Check that they are comfortable, lighting and heating are adequate, and safety and housekeeping issues have been dealt with.

◆ Indicate the rough length of your presentation.

◆ Tell the audience when you will accept questions – in a formal presentation preferably this should be at the end.

- Check that everyone in the room can hear you and see any visual aids.

- If you are using a microphone, speak at your normal level – you don't need to shout.

When you speak

- Stand so that your audience can see you and keep your head up.

- Avoid prowling – move comfortably but don't start quartering the floor.

- Tell your audience briefly what you are going to talk about.

- Indicate what you want from them.

- Speak slightly more slowly than normal – but not so slowly that it sounds unnatural.

- Vary the pace and tone of your delivery – try to avoid speaking in a monotone.

- Maintain eye contact. If you are using visual aids, continue to face the audience – don't turn your back on them.

- Breathe slowly and steadily, particularly if you feel that you are beginning to panic.

- Keep your notes to hand and use them as a stimulus. Don't read a lecture.

- Scan the audience continually for non-verbal signals that they haven't understood (they look blank, frown, start to tap their fingers, etc.) or that they are losing interest (doodling, yawning, flicking through their papers, etc.). If this happens, regroup – can you miss any of the detail out, can you pose a rhetorical question, can you change the pace of your delivery slightly?

- Stick to the timing and content that you have planned – don't digress.

Watch your audience

If you observe any of the following non-verbal signals, your audience may be moving away from you.

- Shake head back and forth
- Raise eyebrows or eyes to ceiling
- Frown
- Look surprised or astonished
- Look anxious to speak
- Lean back in chair
- Fold arms firmly
- Interrupt.

If this happens, try to vary:

- the pace of the presentation – speed up or slow down
- your tone of voice: if you are you beginning to sound bored your audience will switch off
- the activity – ask your audience to look at handouts for a moment.

As a final resort, if you really believe that you have lost your audience's attention completely, suggest a short break. That will give you both chance to regroup.

> 'I do not object to people looking at their watches when I am speaking. But I strongly object when they start shaking them to make certain they are still going.'

Source: Lord Birkett (1883-1962), English judge, The Observer 1960, quoted in *The Hutchinson Dictionary of Business Quotations*

Dealing with questions and conflict

Speakers often worry about the question and answer, but it plays a critical role in audience understanding and retention and you should encourage it. Experts are divided on whether you should take questions at the start or the end. On the one hand questions help to stimulate the interest of the audience and you are responding to their needs. On the other if you respond to questions on an ad hoc basis, you may lose the direction of your presentation, your timing will go to pieces and you could be led into areas that you don't want to address at this particular time. The decision normally rests on how formal the presentation is, but if you choose to take questions as you go along, try to keep your answers concise so that you can pick up the main thread of your presentation.

Hodgson and Hodgson (1992) suggest that you:

- treat all questions as real and answer them as straightforwardly as possible

- don't treat questioners as stupid or frivolous. The answer may seem obvious to you but you're (hopefully) an authority on the subject

- don't avoid questions by changing the subject.

If you don't know the answer, be honest about it.

Questions fall into a number of different types:

1. **Requests for more information** – these are straightforward and you will hopefully be able to answer them immediately. If you don't have the information to hand, make it clear when and how it will be supplied.

2. **Aggressive questions** – these are designed to attack your position or illustrate shortfalls in your argument. They are never easy to deal with but you can counteract them by refusing to rise to the bait. Never lose your temper, reply with a retort or sarcasm or attempt to dismiss the question. If the questioner appears to be looking for an argument, suggest that you discuss the point in more detail after the presentation.

3. **Destructive questions** – these are designed to attack you personally, to make the questioner look smart and you look ineffective. Again, you should never rise to these questions, respond with sarcasm or ignore them. You may find it is effective to ask the questioner if they can elaborate on the points they are making. If an audience member has asked a negative question to embarrass you, they will rarely be able to substantiate it. If the questioning persists, suggest that you continue the discussion later.

After the presentation

As with all types of communication, it is essential to get feedback on your presentation. This will help you to prepare and deliver future presentations.

- Did you fulfil your objective?
- Did you maintain your audience's attention?
- Did they understand the points that you made?
- Has a satisfactory outcome been achieved (i.e. future action agreed)?
- Did your visual aids add to your presentation?
- Was the venue appropriate?

You can collect feedback:

- formally, by asking your audience to complete a brief questionnaire

- by asking for feedback online or by email when you send out notes
- informally by talking to a couple of audience members that you trust to give an honest opinion
- by evaluating your own 'gut reaction' to the presentation. How do you feel that it went?

Activity 10
Collect feedback on your presentation

Self check

Use this self-assessment test to evaluate your own performance before, during and after your presentation.

Use the following scale

1 = very poor, I feel that I performed badly

2 = poor, needed to do more

3 = OK

4 = good, though still room for improvement

5 = very good

	1	2	3	4	5
Before the presentation					
Defined objective of presentation	☐	☐	☐	☐	☐
Chose appropriate time	☐	☐	☐	☐	☐
Chose appropriate venue	☐	☐	☐	☐	☐
Checked layout and facilities in venue	☐	☐	☐	☐	☐
Selected/created appropriate visual aids	☐	☐	☐	☐	☐
Wrote outline for presentation that could be used as a prompt	☐	☐	☐	☐	☐
During the presentation					
Gave a clear introduction	☐	☐	☐	☐	☐
Indicated length of presentation	☐	☐	☐	☐	☐
Told audience when questions would be taken	☐	☐	☐	☐	☐
Checked everyone could see/hear	☐	☐	☐	☐	☐
Monitored audience's non-verbal signals to gauge their interest	☐	☐	☐	☐	☐
Maintained eye contact with range of people in audience	☐	☐	☐	☐	☐
Used accessible language	☐	☐	☐	☐	☐

Varied tone and pace of speech	☐	☐	☐	☐	☐
Used appropriate humour, rhetorical questions, etc.	☐	☐	☐	☐	☐
Answered questions	☐	☐	☐	☐	☐
Focused on predefined content and was not sidetracked	☐	☐	☐	☐	☐
Finished within allotted time	☐	☐	☐	☐	☐
After the presentation					
Devised a mechanism for collecting feedback	☐	☐	☐	☐	☐
Asked audience members for feedback	☐	☐	☐	☐	☐

If you have scored less than 4 for a response, this suggests an area in which you could improve. Look for specific ways to change your presentations and increase your skills – and remember that careful preparation will help to build your confidence when you are speaking.

Next time I will:

Feedback

This activity highlights the importance of careful evaluation after a presentation. It is only through critically reviewing what you have done that you will find ways to improve. Don't be afraid to ask colleagues for their feedback – few people want to criticise unnecessarily and most will look for ways to comment constructively.

◆ Recap

Consider factors that will help you to deliver the presentation effectively, adapting to circumstances as relevant and responding appropriately to questions

◆ Review own performance, and develop own presentation skills accordingly.

Prepare to deliver a presentation by defining your objectives, analysing the audience and any constraints that might impact on your performance

◆ It is essential to define the objectives of your presentation. Why are you giving it, what do you want to achieve and are you the best person to deliver it?

Plan a presentation (including logistics, style, structure, content and media)

◆ A presentation should be designed to appeal to the audience. You should therefore consider their needs when determining what you will say, where and when you will say it and the type of visual aids you will use.

◆ The presentation should follow a logical structure so that it clearly states its intentions at the beginning and ends with a summary of key points.

◆ Timing is important. An audience's attention span starts high, drops quite shallowly for the first 10 minutes, then more steeply until it reached its lowest point after about 30 minutes. Towards the end, it starts to rise again. The structure of the presentation should reflect these highs and lows.

Factors that will help you to deliver the presentation effectively, adapting to circumstances as relevant and responding appropriately to questions

◆ Although public speaking can be a challenge for many people, careful preparation will reduce the risk of losing the thread of your argument or 'drying up'.

◆ Vary the pace and tone of your voice when you can. Use humour if it is appropriate – but be sparing. This is a formal business presentation, not a chance to perform stand-up comedy.

◆ As in any interpersonal communication, it is essential to monitor the audience's non-verbal signals. Look for signs that they are getting bored or confused and alter the pace of the presentation accordingly.

◆ If possible, take questions at the end of the presentation. Treat all questions seriously and with respect, even if you know that the questioner is trying to upset you.

◆ Never try to bluff. If you don't know the answer to a question, admit it and state how you will get the information.

Review own performance, and develop own presentation skills accordingly

◆ Improving your presentation skills is a continual process. Ask audience members for feedback and look for ways to improve the content, pace and style.

▶▶ More @

To develop your presentation skills further, try any of the following texts:

Walters, L. (1993) *Secrets of Successful Speakers*, McGraw Hill Inc.

Bradbury, A. (2006), *Successful Presentation Skills*, Kogan Page

Weismann, J. (2006) *Presenting to Win*, Prentice Hall

Leigh, A. and Maynard, M. (1993) *Perfect Communications*, Arrow Business Books, London

www.businessballs.com has useful sections on making presentations and using visual aids.

5   Interviewing

This is a skill for which many of us receive little training; there is an assumption that anyone who has been through an interview will automatically be able to interview others. This is a misconception: conducting an effective interview that achieves predefined objectives requires particular communication skills. The way in which you use these skills will vary according to the type of interview you are involved in; for example, you will use a different approach in appraisal and selection interviews.

In this section, you will:

♦ examine the range of uses for interviews

♦ plan and prepare for an interview to meet specific situations/objectives and ensure that they are conducted effectively, lawfully and ethically

♦ investigate methods for recording relevant information and outcomes and providing feedback during and following an interview.

Listen

Too many interviewers fail to get a good picture of their interviewee because they have not listened properly. An interview is your opportunity to understand what makes someone else tick and if appropriate to support them to get where they want to go.

Marcus Buckingham in his book about the world's greatest managers, *First break all the rules*, identifies four things to look for – talents, specifics, clues and what a top performer would say. The process looks like this.

Ask a few open-ended questions and then try to keep quiet. The best way to discover a person's *talents* in an interview is to allow him to reveal himself by the choices he makes.

Listen for specifics, past behaviour is a predictor of future behaviour – ask questions like, 'Tell me about a time when …' Listen to their first and immediate response to this and believe it.

Look for clues to talent. Listen for 'a sudden glimpse of excellence at the role, a yearning towards certain activities, a feeling of flow'.

Know what to listen for. As Marcus Buckingham puts it, 'the question is not nearly as important as knowing the best answer.' So if you have a favourite question use it but only if you know how a top performer would respond.

They are all about listening attentively and intently so as not to miss the clues. Your questions are only there to stimulate responses that are sincere and reflect the real person. If you spend too long talking, chances are you will miss the opportunity to really find out what someone is like. Remember they will also want to find out something about the company, your expectations, the way you think too.

Types of interview

Think about the interviews that you have been involved in (either as the interviewer or interviewee) during your career. What was the objective of each type of interview?

In a **selection interview**, the employer collects information about a candidate to find out if they can do the job and will fit in with the organisation. At the same time, the candidate will gather information about the organisation and the job to determine whether this is a position they want.

Appraisal interviews include two components: **performance review** and **development review**. Some companies schedule these separately and some combine them into a general appraisal interview. In a performance review interview, the interviewer wants to identify what progress an individual employee has made during a specified review period and what achievements can be anticipated in the future. At the same time, the interviewee is clarifying what the organisation expects of him or her, and ways in which these expectations can be met. Development review interviews focus on the employee's potential and how it can be enhanced through development and training. The employees uses this process to find out what professional development and job satisfaction the organisation is offering.

Competence interviews address underperformance. The interviewer will try to find out why the interviewee is not meeting targets or experiencing problems, and seek ways to improve their performance. The interviewee will (hopefully) find ways in which the organisation can help them to address their problems.

Disciplinary interviews take place when a there is evidence of employee misconduct and are part of an organisation's clearly defined, written disciplinary process. The aim of disciplinary action should be to improve future conduct but if this doesn't happen, an employee may be dismissed. It is essential that you don't get involved in disciplinary interviews unless you:

◆ have been fully trained and briefed in the relevant procedures

◆ are familiar with employment regulations relating to disciplinary and dismissal procedures

◆ have cleared the interview with senior management before it takes place

◆ know what to record during and after the interview.

In a disciplinary interview, the interviewee will be looking for clear direction about what happens next, particularly if their problems at work persist.

In larger organisations, trained professionals will deal with serious discipline issues. If you don't have this resource, and have to carry out the interviews yourself, research the disciplinary interview process thoroughly before you start and try to involve a third party as a witness and/or mediator. The ACAS website is a useful starting point.

In a **conflict interview**, the interviewer mediates in a dispute between colleagues and looks for ways to move the situation forward by defining clear objectives for both parties. The interviewees will be looking for guidance to resolve their dispute – and will probably also want a chance to air their grievances. In serious disputes, formal organisational procedures may again be invoked, so this is another situation where specialist training is desirable.

Exit interviews take place when an employee is leaving the organisation because they are retiring, have been made redundant or been dismissed. They may combine a degree of paperwork and procedures with some counselling. In a large organisation, the human resource department will conduct these – but if a member of your team is leaving you will probably still want to talk to them and discuss their future plans. Depending on the circumstances in which they are leaving, as well completing any formal leaving procedures, the interviewee may be looking for an acknowledgment of the contribution they've made to the organisation during their period of employment.

Note that in all these types of interview, we have highlighted the expectations of both interviewer and interviewee. Interviews are a two-way process from which both parties should gain.

Interview styles

Holmes (1999) defines three interview styles:

◆ Structured interviews that follow a set format. The interview will ask the same questions in the same order to a number of different people.

◆ Semi-structured interviews. These are less formal although the interviewer will still have a clearly defined purpose. There is more flexibility in the way that questions can be asked.

◆ Unstructured interviews encourage dialogue. Although they will still have an agenda and be used to gather certain information, interviewees will be encouraged to talk freely.

This table illustrates when different types of interview might be appropriate and summarises their advantages and disadvantages.

Style	Example	Advantages	Disadvantages
Structured	Market research Telephone interviews	Systematic, can be used to collect and compare information from a lot of people	Little rapport between interviewer and interviewee No real dialogue
Semi-structured	Selection Appraisal	Clear objectives can be achieved Good for exchanging ideas	Rely heavily on interviewer's communication skills Can be time-consuming
Unstructured	Competence Development review Exit	Can reveal valuable insights and create strong rapport	Information gathered may be hard to categorise Both interviewer and interviewee may move away from the point Can be subjective and unfair

Table 5.1 *Style of interviewing*

A structured interview is designed to discover all relevant information and assess the competencies of the applicant is an efficient method of focusing on the match between job and candidate. It also means that there is a consistent form to the interviews, particularly important if there are a number of candidates to be seen.

Unstructured interviews are very poor for recruiting the right person. The structured interview is most likely to be effective in obtaining specific information against a set of clearly defined criteria. However, not every manager is skilled at interviewing, and may not be able to judge efficiently the applicant's skills and competencies. Ideally all interviewers should receive training, including the equal opportunities aspects of recruitment and the relevant legislation.

Source: www.acas.co.uk

There is no 'ideal' interview style. The way in which you conduct an interview will depend on what you want to achieve, the time and resources available, the culture in your organisation and your own preferred style.

In some situations, particularly during the recruitment and selection processes, different styles of interview may be combined. For example:

◆ All candidates may take part in a telephone interview where information is gathered about their background, qualifications and experience.

◆ Candidates who get through the telephone interview will progress to the next stage where they go through a structured interview. In large organisations these are often rolled into assessment centres where the skills and aptitudes of a number of candidates are tested through a series of exercises. All candidates take the same tests and work through the same challenges. During face-to-face interviews, they will answer the same questions.

◆ The final stage for successful candidates will be an unstructured interview where they talk less formally with prospective employers and may spend time with a number of different people within the organization. At this point, the candidate will be assessed more on their personality. The prospective employer will be looking for evidence that they will fit into the organisation's culture and make a valuable contribution.

Effective interview questioning

There are certain preparatory tasks that you must complete, regardless of the type or style of the interview.

Firstly, you need to clarify your objectives. What do you want to achieve? This will influence the questions that you ask during the interview. You should then prepare questions that relate to your objectives, bearing in mind that your prime objective is to find out what they think and not to hog time with complex questions. If you are involved in a competence-based interview, then the questions may already be drafted out for you. Otherwise you should aim for a balance between different questions types.

Thomson (1998) cites four main types of question that are appropriate for all types of interview:

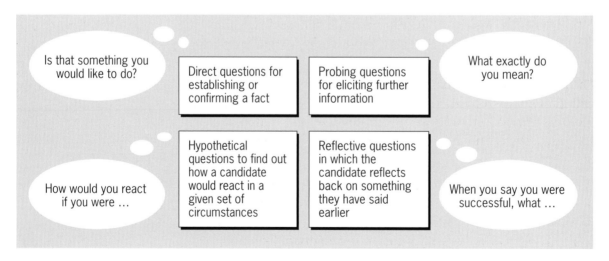

Figure 5.1 *Question types*

This table summarises the pros and cons of using different question styles in an interview.

Type of question	Pros	Cons
Direct	Can be used to establish facts Good for collecting information	Don't encourage the interviewee to open up Don't encourage dialogue
Probing	Good for getting in-depth information Can help to establish dialogue/rapport	You may talk too much May introduce contentious issues Conversation may move away from the job
Hypothetical	Can indicate how interviewee would approach a problem Useful for evaluating skills	Can be unnerving for the interviewee They may not give a truthful answer
Reflective	Good for getting in-depth information Can help to establish dialogue/rapport	Interview may become a conversation You may wander away from the point

Table 5.2 *Question styles in an interview*   Adapted from Holmes (1999)

Questions to avoid and why

It is illegal to discriminate against people on the grounds of sex, race, disability, sexual orientation, and religion or belief – and this includes asking discriminatory questions.

Under the provisions of the Sex Discrimination Act 1975, it is unlawful to discriminate:

◆ In arrangements made for determining who should be offered employment

◆ In terms and conditions of employment

◆ In refusing or deliberately omitting to offer employment on the ground of sex

◆ In preventing access to promotion, training, transfer or any other benefits, facilities or services.

The Race Relations Act states that individuals should not be discriminated against because of their colour, race, ethnic or national origin.

The Disability Discrimination Act 1995 provides disabled people with protection from discrimination, including in recruitment and access to promotion. In terms of recruitment or promotion, an individual should not be treated less favourably because of their disability.

From October 2006, individuals will be protected against age discrimination. This will impact on recruitment and selection procedures and you should use the same care in dealing with age-related issues as you do with gender, race and disability.

The law specifies two types of discrimination:

◆ Direct discrimination in which an individual is clearly disadvantaged because of their sex, race or religion

◆ Indirect discrimination when an organization imposes conditions, not directly related to the job, that only certain people can satisfy. For example, if you quizzed female applicants about their childcare provision but didn't ask male applicants the same questions, you could be guilty of indirect discrimination.

A question may be deemed discriminatory if it relates to the candidate's personal life rather than their work, or if only a few candidates are asked the question. This is one of the reasons why it is particularly important to plan questions in advance; if you have developed a rapport with the interviewee it is easy to make an inappropriate comment.

As a general rule, avoid asking any questions that relate to the interviewee's:

◆ sex or sexual orientation

◆ marital status

◆ race or national origin

◆ physical fitness (unless it is directly relevant to the job).

As well as questions that might result in discrimination, you should also avoid leading questions and multiple questions.

Leading questions: 'It seems to me that this is an example of performing over and above the requirements of the role. Wouldn't you agree?'

Multiple questions which confuse the candidate: 'In the example you just outlined would you say you showed strong problem solving skills and what lessons did you learn about yourself for the future?'

Preparing for the interview

As well as preparing questions, there are a number of other tasks you should complete before the interview.

◆ Make sure the interviewee knows the time, venue and roughly how long the interview will last.

◆ Check that the interview location is suitable – it should be accessible to all interviewees, including those with disabilities. Make sure that the room is booked and you will not be disturbed during the interview.

◆ Think about seating arrangements, particularly if you are organising a panel interview where a number of people will be involved. Pease and Pease (2004) suggest that the desk/chair position can generate an atmosphere that is competitive, defensive or co-operative.

◆ Collect relevant documentation. For a selection interview, this would include the job description, selection criteria, details of any scoring system that should be applied to interviewees, the interviewee's completed application form or CV, the results of any tests they have completed and references if these have already been sent for. In an appraisal interview, you'll need the details of the interviewee's previous appraisal and any performance targets that have been set for them.

◆ Consider how you will record the proceedings. If you intend taking notes while the interviewee is in the room, keep them as brief as possible otherwise long – and embarrassing – silences can develop. Some interviewees will find it intimidating to watch you write about them so if possible, wait until after the interview has finished. Are there forms that you need to complete? If so, study these before the interview so that you are familiar with their demands. Remember that interviewees can ask to see any notes you've made about them so stick to the facts and don't include any wisecracks or potentially offensive remarks.

◆ Determine what feedback you will give during the interview. This will depend on the type of interview. For example, you won't be expected to give an immediate decision at the end of a selection interview. You may, however, be expected to give comprehensive feedback during an appraisal, exit or counselling interview.

Activity 11
Plan and prepare for an interview

Objective

In this activity you will prepare for an interview of any type listed at the beginning of this section.

Task

1. Make a note of who you are interviewing and for what purpose, then use the checklist to ensure that you have taken care of organisational details: tick the box when you have completed each task.

2. List the information that you need to gather from this interview. If you are carrying out a competence-based interview, you may have a pre-prepared list of questions. If so, make a note of the main types of information they focus on.

3. Think about how you will record the interview – taking notes, completing a prep-prepared form, etc. – and what feedback you will give to the interviewee as you talk to them.

4. Give two examples of questions of each type that you could use during the interview. They should be relevant to the interviewee and the subject you are discussing.

Sample questions

Name of interviewee

Purpose of interview

Task	Completed
Interviewee notified of date, time and venue	
Interviewers notified of date, time and venue	
Interview room booked	
Other staff notified that the room will be in use	
Seating arrangements checked	
Relevant paperwork collected	

Information to be gathered during the interview

Methods for recording the interview

Feedback that will be given during the interview

Question type	Examples (two for each type)
Direct	1
	2
Probing	1
	2
Hypothetical	1
	2
Reflective	1
	2

Feedback

Completing this activity should have helped you to structure an interview and to prepare appropriate questions. The more structured the interview, the less likely you are to make random judgements or say something inappropriate. Careful preparation is the most effective way to avoid interview pitfalls.

Interview pitfalls

Interviews must be fair – but, because they are to some degree subjective, it can be difficult to make judgments about people that are not influenced by our own preferences and opinions. Being aware of the interview pitfalls will go some way to helping you make decisions that you may later regret. Try to keep your views to yourself and focus on getting the right person for the job.

The main interview pitfalls are as follows.

♦ **Making a snap judgement** based on someone's appearance, manner or mode of speech. Psychologists have carried out tests to determine how quickly we sum people up when we first meet them – and estimate that we sometimes make decisions about others in as little as 60 seconds. Yes, first impressions can be important – but they can also mislead.

♦ **Mirroring** when you subconsciously favour someone who is like yourself in background, appearance or behaviour. You should also avoid rejecting someone automatically because they resemble a person that you dislike or distrust.

♦ **Superficiality** when an interview becomes so informal that it degenerates into a chat. You may establish good rapport, but find out little of value about the candidate's abilities.

♦ **Logical error** when you make assumptions about an individual's abilities because of things they have done in the past. A person who spent their gap year travelling isn't necessarily intrepid and open to new experiences: they may have hated the experience and come back with firmly entrenched views about other cultures.

♦ **The fatigue factor** when you interview too many people in one session. As you get more tired, you will have less patience and may not be as tolerant of interviewees.

♦ **Talking too much**. A good interviewer listens rather than talks. Your aim is to find out about the interviewee and their ability to do the job, not to impress them.

♦ **Using jargon** or language that the interviewee cannot be expected to understand. This can be intimidating and won't encourage the interviewee to respond.

Feedback after the interview

Perhaps one of the hardest aspects of a manager's job is turning people down. Telling them that they haven't got the job/got a pay rise/performed adequately, demands mature communication skills so that bad news can be conveyed without making the interviewee feel like a total failure.

Giving positive feedback verbally or in writing, outside of a controlled list of reasons, requires a certain level of skill, so that the feedback is not perceived as a criticism, and so that the discussion or communication (whether verbal or a written response) remains adult-to-adult. Written feedback is safer, but verbal feedback is better, if handled well. The risk is that the feedback leads to defence or argument from the recipient, so it's important to accentuate the positive and be objective and factual...

Source: www.businessballs.com

Increasingly interviewees now ask for feedback when they have been unsuccessful in an interview. If you are giving feedback you may want to use these guidelines.

◆ Focus on positive aspects of their performance. 'We were really impressed by...' 'Your experience at ... was very interesting...', 'You did extremely well in the assessment center,' etc.

◆ Keep your remarks impersonal – focus on work-related skills and aptitudes rather than making personal comments. 'Although you've done some work in this field, you would need more experience before we could take you on,' is a more positive response than, 'We didn't think you'd fit it.' It also gives the interviewee something to work towards.

◆ Relate reasons for rejection to the job description.

◆ Maintain confidentiality. Don't refer to anything that was said either by other members of the interview panel or by referees.

What's the future of interviewing?

Here's something to think about. We are increasingly using different technologies to keep in touch. How could you be using technology in the interview process? Think about appraisals, disciplinaries, recruitment and media interviews. Could you be using different media in the future?

How could different media contribute to the different stages in the process?

◆ Recap

Explain the range of uses for interviews

- ◆ Interviews take place for many different reasons: recruitment and selection, performance and development reviews, competence assessment, disciplinary and conflict resolution, and when people leave the organization.

- ◆ Interviews may be structured, semi-structured or unstructured; each type is appropriate for different circumstances.

Plan and prepare for an interview an interview to meet specific situations/objectives and ensure that they are conducted interviews effectively, lawfully and ethically

- ◆ Clarify your objectives – what do you want to achieve? What do you need to find out during the interview?

- ◆ You must be familiar with equal opportunities legislation that affects employment. It is illegal to discriminate against people on the grounds of sex, race, disability, sexual orientation or religion/beliefs.

- ◆ Be aware of interview pitfalls such as making snap judgements, mirroring, superficiality and talking too much.

Recording relevant information and outcomes

- ◆ Before the interview, establish what records you need to keep. Take notes discreetly, and remember that interviewees can ask to see your comments. Keep records secure and make sure they are only accessed by authorized members of staff.

Providing feedback during and following an interview

- ◆ Always be prepared to offer feedback to an interviewee.

- ◆ Be constructive and give them information that will help them in future interviews.

- ◆ Look for aspects of their performance that you can praise.

- ◆ Avoid making personal criticisms.

▶▶ More @

Try any of the following for more on interview techniques

Buckingham, M. (1999) *First Break all the Rules*, Pocket Books

Civil, J. (1997) *Taking Appraisals and Interviews*, Ward Lock

Holmes, K. (1999) *Interviews and Appraisals*, Orion Business Books

Edenborough, R. (2002) *Effective Interviewing: A Handbook of Skills and Teachniques*, Kogan Page

Thomson, R. (1998*) People Management*, Orion Business Books

www.businessballs.com

References

Barker, A. (2000) *Improve Your Communication Skills*, Kogan Page

Berne, E. (1968) *Games People Play*, Penguin

Bonaventura, M. (1997) 'The Benefits of a Knowledge Culture', *AslibProceedings*, Vol. 49, No. 4, 82–89

Buckingham, M. (1999) *First Break all the Rules*, Pocket Books

Ed. Cresswell, J. and Leinster, A. (1996) *The Hutchinson Dictionary of Business Quotations*, Helicon Publishing

Dixon, R. (2003) *The Management Task*, Butterworth Heinemann

Fishenden, J. (1997) 'Managing Intranets to Improve Business Process', *AslibProceedings*, Vol. 49, 4, April, pp.90–96

Guirdham, M. (1995) *Interpersonal Skills at Work*, Prentice Hall

Hodgson, P. and Hodgson, J. (1992) *Effective Meetings*, Century Business

Holmes, K. (1999) *Interviews and Appraisals*, Orion Business Books

Johnson, G. and Scholes, K. (2002) *Exploring Corporate Strategy*, Pearson Education

Joseph, A. (1998) *Put it in Writing, Learn how to Write Clearly, Quickly and Persuasively*, Mcgraw Hill

Leigh, A. and Maynard, M. (1993) *Perfect Communications*, Arrow Business Books

Liebenau, J. and Backhouse, J. (1990) *Understanding Information*, MacMillan

Morling, J. (2000) 'Share or else', *Consultants' Advisory*, December, 30–32

Murdock, A. and Scutt, C. N. (2003) *Personal Effectiveness*, Butterworth Heinemann

Newing, R. (2000) 'Knowledge economy', *Consultant's Adviser*, Iss. 3, 2–4

Nonaka, I. and Takeuchi, H. (1995) *The Knowledge-Creating Company: How Japanese Companies Create the Dynamics of Innovation*, Oxford University Press

Pease, A. and Pease, B. (2004) *The Definitive Book of Body Language*, Orion

Prensky, M. (2001) *Digital Game-Based Learning*, McGraw Hill

Swan, W., Langford, N., Watson, I. and Varey, R. J. (2000) 'Viewing the corporate community as a knowledge network', *Corporate Communications*, Vol. 5, Pt. 2, 97–106

Taylor, S. (2000) *Essential Communication Skills*, Longman

Truss, L. (2005) *Eats Shoots & Leaves*, Profile Books

Von Krogh, G., Ichijo, K. and Nonaka, I. (2000) *Enabling Knowledge Creation: How to Unlock the Mystery of Tacit Knowledge and Release the Power of Innovation,* Oxford University Press

Walters, L. S. (1993) *Secrets of successful speakers*, McGraw Hill Inc.

Willard, N. (1999) 'Knowledge Management: foundations for a secure structure', *Managing Information*, June, 45–49

Websites

www.acas.co.uk

www.businessballs.com

www.channel4.com

www.identity-theft,org.uk

www.london.gov.uk

www.mindtools.com

www.guardian.co.uk